SIMPLY

Crochet

22 STYLISH DESIGNS FOR EVERY DAY

Robyn Chachula

INTERWEAVE
interweave.com

Editor Katrina Loving
Technical Editor Karen Manthey
Art Director Liz Quan
Cover & Interior Design Julia Boyles
Technical Illustrations Robyn Chachula
Glossary Illustrations Ann Swanson
Photography Joe Hancock
Photo Styling Jessica Shinyeda
Production Katherine Jackson

Interweave Press LLC
201 East Fourth Street
Loveland, CO 80537-5655 USA
interweave.com

Printed in China by C&C Offset

Library of Congress
Cataloging-in-Publication Data

Chachula, Robyn, 1978-
Simply crochet : 22 stylish designs for every day / Robyn Chachula.
p. cm.
ISBN 978-1-59668-298-6 (pbk.)
1. Crocheting--Patterns. I. Title.
TT825.C3785 2012
746.43'4--dc23
2011024389

10 9 8 7 6 5 4 3 2 1

ACKNOWLEDGMENTS

I am very thankful for this opportunity to work with such talented and creative designers. Their passion for crochet fueled my love of swatching, drawing diagrams, and even editing. Thank you for making this book come alive with your brilliant projects.

All the yarns used in the book were graciously donated by the yarn companies. Thank you so much for all your support and quick response to my requests; I truly appreciate all that you have given me. Those companies are: Blue Sky Alpacas, Brown Sheep Company, Cascade Yarns, Tahki/Stacy Charles, Lion Brand, Caron International, Spud and Chloe, and Coats & Clark.

Thank you to everyone at Interweave, especially Katrina Loving and Karen Manthey, for making the ramblings of a sleep-deprived mom sound intelligent.

Most important, I would like to thank my friends and family for all their love and support in every crazy challenge I take on. I would especially like to thank my husband, Mark, for his unwavering love. Without his encouragement and help, this book would not have been possible.

Lastly, I want to thank you, the readers. Thank you for enjoying what I love to do so much. Your enthusiasm for crochet is what keeps me energized to share my kooky designs!

DEDICATION

This book is dedicated to my sister, Courtney, for being my constant cheerleader, wise advisor, and comforting friend.   ✳

CONTENTS

INTRODUCTION

Have you ever asked yourself something like "What can I make with this one beautiful ball of yarn?" "Can I really make a shawl with only three balls of yarn?" "Can I make something with scraps from a few old projects?" If you answered yes to any of these questions, then *Simply Crochet* is here to help. This book was designed to give budget-conscious crocheters the tools to make the most of their yarn stashes. Making something yourself is not only satisfying and fun, but it can also save you some money!

When a new baby is born, I immediately start to think about what I can make for him or her (not what I can buy). When I need a gift for teachers, or the mail carrier, or neighbors, I know that crochet is a great way to make a custom gift that won't hurt my pocketbook. The best part is that while you are crocheting all those gifts to show that you care, you will also be having so much fun that you will forget you are saving money. Being frugal does not have to be boring, nor does it mean that you can't be trendy and stylish.

I invite you to start your journey through *Simply Crochet*. There are multiple designers featured in this book to help me show you how to use up every bit of yarn that is sitting around in your craft room, under your sofa, hidden in your car, or forgotten in a closet. Even if you decide to go out and buy new yarn, you'll be delighted with the range of projects in this book that use only a few balls of yarn! The projects are arranged according to the amount of yarn needed. The chapters are broken into one-, three-, and five-ball projects (or fewer). You will see that five balls of yarn really can make a great sweater or a cute baby blanket, while just one ball can yield a stylish cowl or chic hat.

Throughout the book, you'll find tips and tricks for things such as buying yarn on a budget, repurposing old projects for usable yarn, and using remnants of yarn left over from past projects. You'll find that sticking to a budget is easier than it sounds. So, grab your hooks and yarn stash and come along to see what hidden gems we have cooked up for you!

> *Making something yourself is not only satisfying and fun, but it can also save you some money!*

1 BALL
or less

iced ascot

rebecca velasquez

So often we save our "good china" or "good yarn" for special occasions. The unfortunate result is that it is rarely seen and appreciated. Well, this ascot is the perfect reason to break out the good yarn. Combining luxurious alpaca yarn with simple stitches and a relaxed keyhole style creates a beautiful, versatile piece that is equally appropriate for date night or the kids' school play.

MATERIALS

yarn: Sportweight (#2 Fine).

Shown: Blue Sky Alpacas, Royal (100% royal alpaca; 288 yd [263 m]/3.5 oz [100 g]): #708 Seaglass (MC), 1 ball.

hook: F/5 (3.75 mm) or hook needed to obtain gauge.

notions: Tapestry needle for weaving in ends; spray bottle with water and straight pins for blocking.

GAUGE

16 sts by 8 rows = 4" × 4" (10 × 10 cm) in stitch pattern.

FINISHED SIZE

5½" × 51" (14 × 129.5) cm.

{note}

* Ascot is made from center back to left end, rejoin at center, crochet to right end.

pattern

Refer to the **Iced Stitch Pattern** diagram at right for assistance.

Ch 23 with MC.

ROW 1 (RS): Sc in 2nd ch from hook, *ch 3, sk next 2 ch, sc in next ch; rep from * across, turn—7 ch-3 sps.

ROW 2: Ch 3 (counts as dc), dc in first sc, *sc in next ch-3 sp, 3 dc in next sc; rep from * across, ending with 2 dc in last sc, turn.

ROW 3: Ch 1, sc in first dc, *ch 3, sk next 3 sts, sc in next dc; rep from * across, ending with sc in top of tch, turn.

ROWS 4–28: Rep Rows 2–3 twelve times; then rep Row 2 once.

ROW 29: Ch 3 (counts as dc), *sk next 3 sts, dc in next dc; rep from * across, ending with dc in 3rd ch of tch, turn—8 dc.

Create Pull-Through Loop

Back

ROW 30: Ch 1, sc in each dc across, sc in top of tch, turn—8 sc.

ROW 31: Ch 3 (counts as dc), dc-flp in ea sc across, leave tch unworked, turn—8 dc.

ROWS 32–33: Ch 3 (counts as dc), dc in ea dc across, turn—8 dc.

Fasten off.

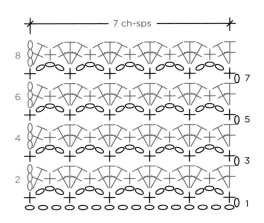

Iced Stitch Pattern Diagram

Front

With RS facing, join yarn to first unused lp of sc row (30), which are now the front lps.

ROWS 31–33: Rep Rows 31–33 of Back. Do not fasten off.

ROW 34: Align the Front and Back piece of the lps so that you can work through both fabrics at the same time. Ch 1, working through double thickness, sc in each dc across. (Hook should pass under the 2 lps for the front piece and 2 lps for the back piece at the same time, in effect "sewing" them together.)

ROW 35: Ch 6, dc in next sc, *ch 3, dc in next sc; rep from * across ending with dc in last sc, turn.

ROW 36: Ch 3, dc in first dc, sc in ch-3 sp. *3 dc in next dc, sc in next ch-3 sp; rep from * across, ending with 2 dc in 3rd ch of tch, turn.

ROW 37: Rep Row 3.

ROWS 38–54: Rep Rows 2–3. Fasten off.

Turn piece so that you may work again into the original foundation chain.

Making certain the right side is facing you, rejoin yarn to first ch.

ROW 55: Ch 3, dc in first ch, sc in ch-2 sp. *3 dc in same ch as sc of Row 1, sc in next ch-2 sp; rep from * across ending with 2 dc in last ch.

ROWS 56–99: Rep Rows 2–3, ending with Row 2 of patt. Fasten off. Weave in all ends.

Finishing

Lightly wet-block to finished measurements, "opening up" scalloped edge.

Rebecca Velasquez is wife to her
Mr. Wonderful and a homeschool-
ing mom of four, living in Amarillo,
Texas. Playing with yarn is her daily
meditation. Her design work for
both crochet and knitting is as much
a necessity to her well-being as it
is a pleasure. Read and see more at
RebeccaVelasquez.com.

If you had only one ball of yarn…
To me, making the most of my
luxury yarn means creating something I will use. I've made fingerless
mitts from one hank of a dreamy
alpaca yarn my husband bought for
me on one of his business trips. A
short, light accessory scarf or cowl is
another option that is both practical
and indulgent.

flapper hat

margaret hubert

I have always been intrigued by the unique styles of the 1920s—especially those fantastic hats! Worn low on the forehead, this perky little hat reminds me of a 1920s cloche, with an offset floral embellishment and a pretty scalloped edge. Crochet a few in different colors to add a feminine vintage-inspired touch to any outfit.

MATERIALS

yarn: Worsted weight (#4 Medium).

Shown: Caron, Simply Soft (100% Acrylic; 157 yd [144 m]/3 oz [85 g]): 1 skein each #9719 soft pink (MC) and #9722 plum wine (CC) (yarn listed is enough to make 2 hats).

hook: H/8 (5 mm) or hook needed to obtain gauge.

notions: Straight pins; tapestry needle for weaving in ends.

GAUGE

12 dc by 6 rows = 4" × 4" (10 × 10 cm).

FINISHED SIZE

Hat fits a 22" (56 cm) head circumference.

{note}

* Crown is worked in the round, border is worked in rows to form a band, then sewn to crown.

pattern

Crown

Ch 5 with MC, sl st in first ch to form ring.

RND 1 (RS): Ch 1, 10 sc in center of ring, join with a sl st to beg ch 1.

RND 2: Ch 3 (counts as dc here and throughout), * 2 dc in next sc, rep from * around, sl st to top of tch, do not turn—21 dc.

RND 3: Ch 3, *dc in next dc, 2 dc in next dc, rep from * around, sl st to top of tch, do not turn—31 dc.

RND 4: Ch 3, *dc in next 2 dc, 2 dc next dc, rep from * around, sl st to top of tch, do not turn—41 dc.

RND 5: Ch 3, *dc in next 3 dc, 2 dc in next dc, rep from * around, sl st to top of tch, do not turn—51 dc.

RND 6: Ch 3, *dc in next 4 dc, 2 dc in next dc, rep from * around, sl st to top of tch, do not turn—61 dc.

RND 7: Ch 3, dc in each dc around, sl st to top of tch, do not turn.

Rep Rnd 7 once. Fasten off.

Bottom Border

Refer to **Stitch Diagram A** above for assistance.

With MC, ch 14.

ROW 1 (WS): Dc in 4th ch from hook, dc in next 4 ch, ch 3, skip next 2 ch, sc in next ch, ch 3, sk next 2 ch, (dc, ch 5, sl st) in last ch, turn.

ROW 2: (Sc, 2 hdc, 5 dc) in next ch-5 sp, dc in next dc, ch 5, skip next 2 ch-3 sps, dc in next dc, ch 4, skip next 4 dc, dc in top of tch, turn.

ROW 3: Ch 3, 4 dc in next ch-4 sp, dc in next dc, ch 3, sc in next ch-5 sp, ch 3, (dc, ch 5, sl st) in next dc, turn, leave rem sts unworked.

Rep Rows 2 and 3 for border patt until piece measures 22″ (56 cm) from beg, ending with Row 2 of patt. Fasten off, leaving a long tail for sewing.

With yarn tail and tapestry needle, without twisting border, whipstitch short ends of Border together. Pin straight edge of Border to Crown, matching seam on Border to tch "seam" on Crown, match center of Border to center front of Crown. Whipstitch Border to Crown, easing in fullness.

Finishing

Fans

Make 1 using CC only; make 3 alternating 2 rows MC and 2 rows CC throughout.

First Segment

Ch 15.

ROW 1: Starting in 2nd ch from hook, sc in next 2 ch, hdc in next 3 ch, dc in next 2 ch, 2 dc in next ch, dc in next 3 ch, tr in next 3 ch, do not turn.

ROW 2: Ch 1, working from left to right, reverse sc in flo of each st across (this completes one section of fan), do not turn.

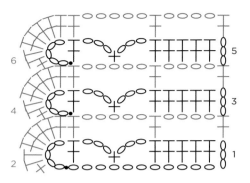

A. Bottom Border

ROW 3: Ch 1, working behind reverse sc row in the free lps not prev worked 2 rows below, sc in next 2 sts, hdc in next 3 sts, dc in next 2 sts, 2 dc in next st, dc in next 3 sts, tr in next 3 sts, do not turn.

ROW 4: Rep Row 2.

ROWS 5–8: Rep Rows 3–4 (twice). Fasten off.

Small Flowers

Make 5 with CC.

Ch 5, sl st to first ch to form ring.

RND 1: *Ch 3, 5 dc in ring, ch 3, sl st in ring, rep from * once. Fasten off, leaving a long tail for sewing. Whipstitch embellishments to hat covering seam sts, referring to the photo on page 14 for placement, or arranging as desired.

Margaret Hubert has knitted and crocheted most of her life, has owned her own yarn shop, and was a needlework instructor for Bloomingdale's. She has been writing knitting and crochet books since 1978 and is currently working on her twentieth book. She loves to teach both knitting and crochet.

If you had only one ball of yarn… I would make a lovely, soft, drapey scarf.

billows of baubles

sheryl means

Imagine light-as-air baubles floating delicately around your neck. That was the vision for this unique piece. The unusual construction of this scarf, paired with a lightweight stainless steel–based yarn, produces an elegant sculptural accessory with infinite possibilities.

{notes}

* The unique nature of this yarn makes it difficult to count complete rows. Use a row counter to mark the end of every return pass.

* Do not worry about the crumpled nature of the work in progress, it is easy to pull into shape.

* The first loop on hook counts as a stitch in all stitch counts.

* When increasing to create a bauble, work Tdc in each tss and in each space between stitches.

* The two scarves are joined during the forward pass of the second and ninth row of the band on the second scarf. To simplify the join, use a locking stitch marker to hold the left sides together as the join is made.

MATERIALS

yarn: Fingering weight (# 1 Super Fine).

Shown: LB Collection, Wool Stainless Steel (75% wool, 25% stainless steel; 273 yd [244 m]/0.50 oz [14 g]): #114 cerise (purple), 1 cone.

hook: I/9 (5.5 mm) Tunisian crochet hook or hook needed to obtain gauge.

notions: Row counter; 1 locking stitch marker; tapestry needle for weaving in ends.

GAUGE

15 sts by 5 rows = 4" × 4" (10 × 10 cm) in Tunisian double crochet. Due to the unique nature of this yarn, an exact gauge is difficult to measure and not significant to the project.

FINISHED SIZE

5" wide x 88" long (12.5 × 223.5 cm) when fully stretched.

schematic

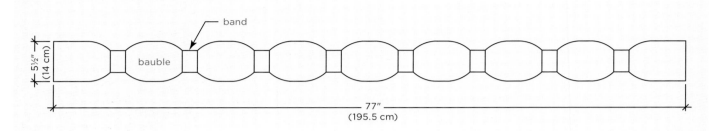

band

bauble

5½"
(14 cm)

77"
(195.5 cm)

details

Special Stitches

Tunisian Simple Stitch (tss): p. 156.

Tunisian Double Crochet (tdc) Fwd:
p. 156.

*Tunisian Simple Stitch 2 together
(tss2tog):* Insert hook under next 2
vertical bars, yo, draw yarn through sts.

Single Crochet Bind-Off: Insert hook
under next vertical bar, yo, draw yarn
through bar, yo, draw through both
loops on hook.

crocheting
on a budget

Hands down, my choice is sock yarn.
Each ball of sock yarn is a surprise
waiting to happen. The yardage is
fabulous, and one ball will make a
substantial project.

✳ *Sheryl Means*

pattern

First Scarf

Refer to **Stitch Diagram A** on page 21
for assistance.

Foundation Bauble

Ch 21.

ROW 1: Tdc in 3rd ch from hook
(skipped chs count as first tdc), tdc in
ea ch across. **RetP**—20 tdc.

ROW 2: Ch 1 (counts as first tdc), tdc in
ea st across, tdc in 2 vertical strands at
top of last st. **RetP**.

Rep Row 2 eight times—10 total rows.

Band

ROW 1: Ch 1, *tss2tog in over next 2 sts,
rep from * to across last st, tss in 2 vertical strands at top of last st. **RetP**—11 tss.

ROW 2: Tss in each st across, tss in
2 vertical strands at top of last st.
RetP—11 tss.

Rep Row 2 eight times—10 total rows.

Bauble

ROW 1: Ch 1, *Tdc in next tss, Tdc in sp
bet sts, rep from * across, ending with

1 Tdc in 2 vertical strands at top of last
st—20 Tdc.

ROW 2: Ch 1, Tdc in each st across,
tdc in 2 vertical strands at top of last
st—20 Tdc.

Rep Row 2 eight times—10 total rows.

Work alternating Bands and Baubles
8 times.

LAST ROW: Work single crochet bind-
off after 10th row. Fasten off; weave in
end.

Second Scarf

Foundation Bauble

Work same as Foundation Bauble of
First Scarf.

Band

ROW 1: Ch 1, *tss2tog over next 2
sts, rep from * to across last st, tss
in 2 vertical strands at top of last st.
RetP—11 tss.

ROW 2: Line up the edge of work with
first Band of First Scarf; sl st in edge
of First Scarf, *tss inserting hook from
front to back under bar bet ea tss and
under corresponding bar on First Scarf,
rep from * across, ending with sl st

in 2 vertical strands at top of last st. **RetP**—11 tss.

ROW 3: Tss in each st across, tss in 2 vertical strands at top of last st. **RetP**—11 tss.

Rep Row 3 six times—9 total rows.

ROW 10: Rep Row 2, joining top Row 9 of corresponding Band of First Scarf.

Bauble

ROW 1: Ch 1, *Tdc in next tss, Tdc in sp bet sts, rep from * across, ending with 1 Tdc in 2 vertical strands at top of last st. **RetP**—20 Tdc.

ROW 2: Ch 1, Tdc ending with 1 Tdc in 2 vertical strands at top of last st. **RetP**—20 Tdc.

Rep Row 2 eight times—10 total rows.

Work alternating Bands and Baubles 8 times.

LAST ROW: Work single crochet bind-off after 10th row. Fasten off; weave in end.

Finishing

Blocking is simply a matter of pulling scarf into shape.

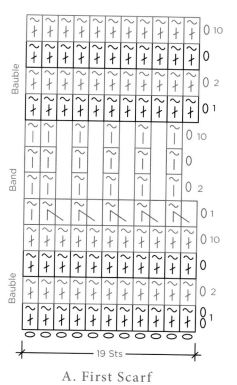

A. First Scarf

Sheryl Means is a yarn shop owner, crochet designer, fiber artist, and maker of fun, funky yarn. Her shop, Yarntopia, is a place for knitters and crocheters to come together and have fun. She is fortunate to have a wide array of yarn available at her shop and loves helping others make their fiber dreams come true. She can be found online at sherylmeanscrochet.com and yarntopia.net.

If you had only one ball of yarn... I am an accessories girl, and I love triangular scarves and wraps. No matter the yardage, I can always find a way to turn it into a triangular treat.

twist cowl/wrap

linda permann

Get the drape and texture you crave with a doubled strand of laceweight yarn and the stretchy Solomon's Knot stitch. This versatile Möbius can be worn a number of ways—as a cowl, a snood, a wrap, or an oversize necklace—and it scrunches up perfectly for travel. Experiment with different yarn weights and textures—each wrap only takes about 275 yards (251 m) of yarn (held single with a thicker yarn) or 550 yards (503 m) of yarn (held double with a laceweight yarn) to crochet.

MATERIALS

yarn: Laceweight (#0 Lace).

Shown: Brown Sheep Company, Legacy Lace (75% washable wool, 25% nylon, 1,500 yd [1376 m]/6 oz [170 g]): #20 golden sunrise, 1 ball (will make at least 2 wraps).

hook: 7 (4.5 mm) or hook needed to obtain gauge. Hook size is not as important as making each loop the correct size, as detailed in Special Stitches.

notions: Tapestry needle.

GAUGE

7 lsk by 6 rows measures 4" × 4" (10 cm × 10 cm) square (unstretched) in Solomon's Knot Pattern.

FINISHED SIZE

About 44" around × 14" wide laid flat (with twist; 112 × 35.5 cm). Wrap is very stretchy and will accommodate a range of sizes. See Note in pattern about changing length of wrap for smaller or larger shoulder width.

{notes}

* Wrap is constructed as one long rectangle, then twisted and joined as you go along short sides.

* Yarn is held double throughout the pattern.

details

Special Stitches

Edge Solomon's Knot (esk): Draw lp on hook to about ½" (1.3 cm) in length, yo and draw the lp through the long lp.

Long Solomon's Knot (lsk): Draw lp on hook to about 1" (2.5 cm) in length, yo and draw the lp through the long lp.

Back Loop (blp): The back lp is the single strand of the Solomon's Knot made from the yo, the double strand is the front lp made from drawing up a lp.

pattern

Refer to the **Solomon's Knot Stitch Pattern** diagram below right for assistance.

Ch 2.

ROW 1: Sc in 2nd ch from hook, [esk, sc in blp of esk] 24 times—24 esk.

ROW 2: lsk, sc in blp of lsk, turn, sk 2 esk, sc in next sc, *[lsk, sc in blp of lsk] twice, skip 2 esk, sc in next sc; rep from * across—23 lsk.

ROW 3: [esk, sc in blp of esk] twice, turn, (lsk, sc in blp of lsk), sk first lsk of row below, sc in next sc, *[lsk, sc in blp of lsk] twice, skip 2 esk, sc in next sc; repeat from * across—23 esk.

ROWS 4–62: Rep Row 3. Check length of wrap; it should fit comfortably around your shoulders without falling off.

NOTE: Add or subtract rows to achieve desired length, being sure to work an even total number of rows.

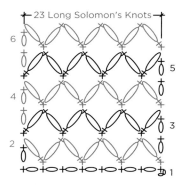

Solomon's Knot Stitch
Pattern Diagram

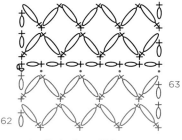

A. Joining Diagram

Linda Permann is a crafty dabbler and the author of *Little Crochet: Modern Designs for Babies and Toddlers* and *Crochet Adorned: Reinvent Your Wardrobe with Crocheted Accents, Embellishments and Trims.* She designs and teaches crochet in San Antonio, Texas. Read about her crafty adventures at lindamade.com.

If you had only one ball of yarn...
I tend to buy special hanks of yarn as souvenirs when I am traveling, and I like to make detailed, time-consuming projects with them so that I can get a lot of enjoyment out of the yarn. I go for lighter weights like sock and lace, because each ball typically has the yardage needed to complete an entire project.

Twist the Wrap

Lay strip flat with working edge toward you. Twist opposite edge (referred to as JE [joining edge]) once and align it with the working edge, preserving the twist.

Refer to **Stitch Diagram A** at bottom left for assistance with joining.

ROW 63 (JOINING ROW): [esk, sc in blp of esk] twice, sl st in first sc of JE, (lsk, sc in blp of lsk), sk lsk and sc in next sc of row below, * (lsk, sc in blp of lsk), sk next sc of JE, sl st in next sc along JE, (lsk, sc in blp of lsk), sk next sc of row below, sc in next sc; rep from * across, esk, sc in blp of esk, sl st in last sc of JE.

Fasten off and weave in the ends. To retain springy nature of knots, do not block.

mystic cuff

robyn chachula

I am a jewelry fiend. It is like candy to me; I just cannot resist. Thank goodness for crochet! The inspiration for this cuff came from a recent trip to my local mall, where I spotted the most adorable bracelet. Knowing that buying it would break my bank, I decided to crochet something similar to quench my desire and add to my collection.

MATERIALS
yarn: Laceweight (#0 Lace).

Shown: (Coats and Clark) Aunt Lydia's, Classic Crochet Thread, Size 10 (100% mercerized cotton; 350 yd [320 m]/3 oz [85 g]): #0622 kelly green (MC), 1 partial skein (25 yd); #0012 black (CC), 1 partial skein (25 yd).

hook: Steel No. 2 (1.5 mm) or hook needed to obtain gauge.

notions: Sewing needle for weaving in ends; spray bottle with water and straight pins for blocking; six 8mm beads; small toggle clasp or 6mm bead for closure.

GAUGE
Finished cuff = 2¼" × 7¾" (5.5 × 19.5 cm).

FINISHED SIZE
2¼" × 7¾" (5.5 × 19.5 cm).

{note}

* When picking out beads, be sure that the hole is at least 2 mm so the bead will fit over the foundation chain.

---

pattern

Cuff

Refer to **Stitch Diagram A** below for assistance.

Ch 52 with MC or CC.

RND 1 (RS): Dc in 5th ch from hook (skipped ch counts as dc), dc in next ch, *ch 5, string bead onto foundation chain (thread bead over entire chain from end and up to last st made) sk next 3 ch, dc in next 5 ch (this will trap the bead bet the sts), rep from * to last 6 ch, ch 5, string bead onto chain, sk next 3 ch, dc in next 2 ch, (3 dc, ch 5, 3 dc) in last ch, rotate cuff 180 degrees and across opposite side of foundation ch, dc in next 2 ch, **ch 5, sk next 3 ch, dc in next 5 ch, rep from ** 4 times, ch 5, sk next 3 ch, dc in next 2 ch, (3 dc, ch 5, 2 dc) in next ch, sl st to top of tch, do not turn—14 ch-sps.

RND 2: Ch 1, sc in top of tch, *(4 dc, ch 2, 4 dc) in next ch-5 sp, sk 2 dc, sc in next dc, sk 2 dc, rep from * 5 times, (5 dc, ch 3, 5 dc) in next ch-5 sp, rotate cuff 180 degrees, sk 2 dc, sc in next dc, rep from * to last ch-5 sp, (5 dc, ch 3, 5 dc) in last ch-5 sp, sl st to first sc, do not turn—14 ch-sps.

RND 3: Sl st in next dc, ch 3, *sk next dc, dc in next dc, ch 1, sk next dc, (dc, ch 2, dc) in next ch-2 sp, ch 1, sk next dc, dc in next dc, ch 1, sk next dc, dc-2tog over next 2 dc (skipping sc bet), ch 1*, rep from * to * 5 times, **(dc, ch 1) in ea of next 4 dc, (dc, ch 2, dc) in next ch-2 sp, ch 1, (dc, ch 1) in ea of next 4 dc, dc2tog over next 2 dc (skipping sc bet), ch 1**, rep from * to * 6 times, rep from ** to ** once, hdc in last dc, sl st to 2nd ch of tch, do not turn—82 ch-sps.

RND 4: Ch 1, ** *(sc, ch 2) in ea of next 2 ch-1 sps, (sc, ch 4, sc) in next ch-2 sp, (ch 2, sc) in ea of next 2 ch-1 sps, ch 2,* rep from * to * 5 times, (sc, ch 2) in ea of next 5 ch-1 sps, (sc, ch 2, sc) in next ch-2 sp, (sc, ch 2) in ea of next 5 ch-1 sps, rep from ** once, sl st to first sc—96 ch-sps. Fasten off.

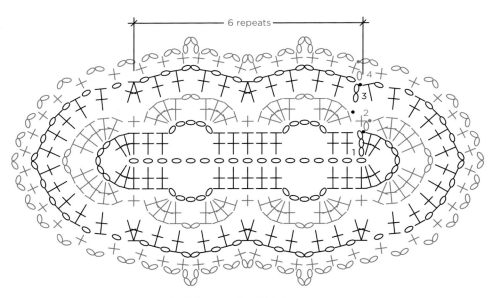

A. Mystic Cuff Diagram

Finishing

Pin cuff to finished size (see Finished Size on page 27). You can vary the look of the cuff by choosing which ch-sps to pin. The green cuff has the center 3 ch-sps on ea curve pinned higher than the valley ch-sps. The black cuff has all the ch-sps equally pinned out and blocked. Spray with water and allow to dry. Sew the toggle half of the clasp or the chosen bead to one end of the cuff; use ch-sp as buttonhole on other end.

emma lace scarf

simona merchant-dest

This gorgeous scarf was inspired by a leather belt with a Victorian motif that I saw in a fashion magazine. The intricate-looking design is actually quite simple to crochet and creates a versatile scarf to complement many an outfit. Wear it wrapped around the neck several times for warmth or wear it looser to show off the pattern.

MATERIALS

yarn: DK weight (#3 Light).

Shown: Lion Brand Yarn, LB Collection Superwash Merino (100% superwash Merino; 306 yd [280 m]/3.5 oz [100 g]): #114 cayenne, 1 ball.

hook: G/6 (4 mm) or hook needed to obtain gauge.

notions: Tapestry needle for weaving in ends; 6 stitch markers (optional); spray bottle with water and straight pins for blocking.

GAUGE

20 dc by 9 rows = 4" × 3" (10 × 7.5 cm) in Center Stitch Pattern.

FINISHED SIZE

7½" × 68" (19 × 173 cm).

{note}

* Scarf is worked in one piece lengthwise in two directions. Starting with foundation single crochet (fsc), scalloped border stitch pattern is worked downward, then center stitch pattern is worked upward from fsc and finished off with scalloped stitch pattern border.

details

Special Stitches

2 Double Crochet Cluster (2dc-cl): p. 155.

Foundation Single Crochet (fsc): p. 154.

Ch-3 Picot (picot): Ch 3, sl st into last sc made.

Modified Ch-3 Picot (MP): Sl st into indicated st, ch 3, sl st in the same indicated st.

Scalloped Border Stitch Pattern (sbsp)

Refer to **Scalloped Border Stitch Pattern** above right for assistance.

Fsc a multiple of 8 plus 2.

ROW 1 (WS): *Ch 3, sk next 2 fsc, sc in next fsc, ch 5, sk next 4 fsc, sc in next fsc; rep from * across to last 2 fsc, ch 1, hdc in last fsc, turn.

ROW 2: Ch 1, sc in first hdc, sk ch-1 sp, *9 dc in next ch-5 sp, sk next sc, sc in next ch-3 sp; rep from * across, turn.

ROW 3: Ch 6 (count as tr and ch 2), sk first sc and next 2 dc, *MP in next dc, sc in ea of next 3 dc, MP in next dc **, ch 5, sk next (2 dc, sc, 2 dc); rep from * across ending last rep at **, ch 2, sk next 2 dc, tr in last sc, turn.

ROW 4: Ch 1, sc in tr, * ch 3, sk next sc, 2 dc in next sc, ch 3, sk next sc, sc in next ch-5 sp **, picot; rep from * across, ending last rep at ** , turn.

ROW 5: * Ch 5, sk sc, sc in next ch-3 sp, ch 3, sk next 2 dc, sc in next ch-3 sp; rep from * across to last sc, ch 2, dc in last sc, turn.

ROW 6: Ch 3 (count as 1 dc), 4 dc in next ch-2 sp, sk next sc, sc in next ch-3 sp, * 9 dc in next ch-5 sp, sk next sc, sc in next ch-3 sp; rep from * across to last ch-5 sp, sk sc, 5 dc in last ch-5 sp.

Center Stitch Pattern (csp)

Multiple of 6 plus 1 sts.

ROW 1 (RS): Ch 3 (count as dc), working across ch side of fsc, dc in next st and in ea fsc across, turn.

ROW 2: Ch 3 (count as hdc and ch 1), sk first 2 dc, *hdc in next dc, ch 1, sk next dc; rep from * across to tch, hdc in top of tch, turn.

ROW 3: Ch 1, sc in first hdc, *sc in next ch-1 sp, sc in next hdc; rep from * across to tch, sc in ea of first 2 ch of tch, turn.

ROW 4: Ch 1, sc in in first sc, *ch 2, sk next 2 sc, (dc, ch 2, dc) in next sc, ch 2, sk next 2 sc, sc in next sc **, picot (see Special Stitches); rep from * across ending last rep at **, turn.

ROW 5: Ch 3, sk (first sc, ch-2 sp and dc), * (2dc-cl, ch 2, 2dc-cl, ch 2, 2dc-cl) in next ch-2 sp **, ch 1, sk (next dc, ch-2 sp, sc, next ch-2 sp, and next dc); rep from * across ending last rep at **, sk next dc and ch-sp, dc in last sc, turn.

ROW 6: Ch 3 (count as hdc and ch 1), sk first 2 sts, *[hdc in next ch-2 sp, ch 1, sk next 2dc-cl] twice **, hdc in next ch-1 sp, ch 1, sk next 2dc-cl; rep from * across ending last rep at **, hdc in top of tch, turn.

ROW 7: Ch 1, sc in first hdc, *sc in next ch-1 sp, sc in next hdc; rep from * across to tch, sc in ea of first 2 ch of tch, turn.

ROW 8: Ch 3 (count as hdc and ch 1), sk first 2 sc, hdc in next sc, ch 1, *sk next sc, ch 1, hdc in next sc; rep from * across, turn.

ROW 9: Ch 3 (count as dc), sk first hdc, *dc in next ch-1 sp, dc in next hdc; rep from * across to tch, dc in ea of next 2 ch of tch.

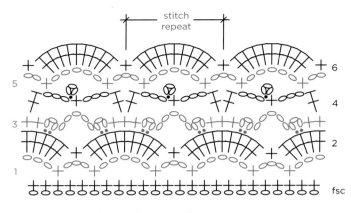

Scalloped Border Stitch Pattern Diagram

pattern

Refer to **Stitch Diagram A** on page 34 for assistance.

Border

Fsc 338.

NOTE: To help with counting stitches, mark every 50th fsc with removable marker.

ROW 1 (WS): Work Row 1 of sbsp, turn—42 ch-5 sps.

ROW 2: Work Row 2 of sbsp, turn—forty-two 9-dc sh.

ROWS 3–6: Work Rows 3–6 of sbsp.

Fasten off.

Center

Turn piece upside down, and with fsc and RS facing, join yarn with sl st in ch side of first fsc.

ROW 1 (RS): Work Row 1 of csp across to last 2 fsc, dc2tog over last 2 sts, turn—337 dc.

ROWS 2–9: Work Rows 2–9 of csp. Fasten off.

Border

FOUNDATION ROW (RS): With RS facing, join yarn in top ch of tch, ch 1, sc in top ch of same tch, sc in next and ea dc across to last dc, 2 sc in last dc—338 sc.

ROW 1: Work Row 1 of sbsp, turn—42 ch-5 sps.

ROW 2: Work Row 2 of sbsp, turn—forty-two 9-dc sh.

ROWS 3–6: Work Rows 3–6 of sbsp.

Fasten off.

Finishing

Edging

With RS facing, join yarn to right corner of the short edge.

ROW 1: Ch 1, sc evenly across edge, turn.

ROW 2: Ch 2 (count as hdc), sk first sc, hdc in next and ea sc across, turn.

ROW 3: Ch 1, sc in first and ea hdc across, turn.

Rep Rows 2–3 twice more.

Fasten off and weave in loose ends.

Rep Edging across other short side of scarf.

Pin to finished measurements. Spritz with water and allow to dry.

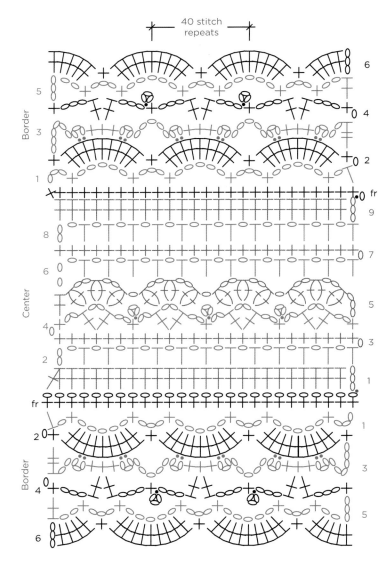

A. Emma Lace Scarf Diagram

Simona Merchant-Dest loves fashion and designs both knit and crochet garments and accessories. She has worked as design director and project coordinator for Mission Falls books. You can see more of her work at SimonaMerchantDest.com. She blogs at StylishKnits.blogspot.com.

If you had only one ball of yarn…
I tend to display it on my shelf in the office so I can enjoy it first. Then I look for a special stitch pattern to make a scarf or hat.

diamonds and lace hat

linda permann

Play with texture and lace in this sweetly patterned beanie. Diamonds edged in chain spaces and post stitch cables wind up to the crown to converge in openwork shaping that resembles the sun's rays. Worked in a fine sock-weight yarn, this hat provides warmth and style without a lot of bulk. For something entirely different, try it in a self-striping sock yarn with long repeats or choose solid and tonal yarns to really show off your stitch work.

MATERIALS

yarn: Fingering weight (#1 Super Fine).

Shown: Spud and Chloe, Fine (80% wool, 20% silk; 248 yd [227 m]/2.25 oz [65 g]): #7814 shitake, 1 ball.

hook: C/2 (2.75 mm) or hook needed to obtain gauge.

notions: Tapestry needle; spray bottle with water and T-pins for blocking.

GAUGE

16 sts by 10 rows = 3″ × 3″ (7.5 × 7.5 cm) square, worked in stitch pattern.

FINISHED SIZE

Hat measures 19½″ (49.5 cm) in circumference at brim, but will stretch to fit 22–23″ (56–58.5 cm) head circumference.

details

Special Stitches

Foundation Double Crochet (fdc):
Yo, insert hook in 3rd ch from hook, yo and pull up a lp (3 lps on hook). Yo and draw through first lp (1 ch made), [yo and draw through 2 lps] twice (dc made)—1 fdc made. For subsequent stitches, yo and insert hook under 2 lps of chain just made, yo and draw a lp through the ch (ch made), [yo and draw through 2 lps on hook] twice.

Left Leaning Front Post Double Crochet Decrease (FPdecL): Yo, insert hook from front to back to front around post of st below, yo and draw up a lp, yo and draw through 2 lps on hook; yo, insert hook in next st, yo and draw up a lp, yo and draw lp through 2 lps on hook once, yo and draw lp through rem 3 lps on hook.

Right Leaning Front Post Double Crochet Decrease (FPdecR): Yo, insert hook in next st, yo and draw up a lp, yo and draw lp through 2 lps on hook; yo, insert hook from front to back to front around post of next st below, yo and draw up a lp, yo and draw through 2 lps on hook, yo and draw lp through rem 3 lps on hook.

Front Post Double Crochet 3 Together (FPdc3tog): (Yo, insert hook from front to back to front around post of next designated st below, yo and draw up a lp, yo and draw through 2 lps on hook) 3 times, yo and draw through all 4 lps on hook.

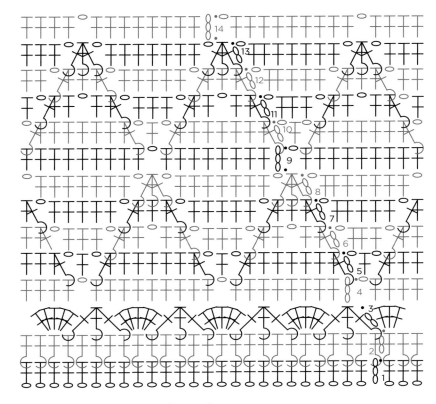

Diamond Stitch Pattern Diagram

pattern

Refer to the **Diamond Stitch Pattern** diagram above for assistance.

RND 1: Ch 3 (counts as first Fdc), Fdc 101, join with sl st in beginning ch, being careful not to twist—102 Fdc.

RND 2: Ch 2 (does not count as a st here or throughout), *FPdc in next st, BPdc in next st; rep from * around, join with sl st in first FPdc—51 FPdc, 51 BPdc.

RND 3: Ch 2, *FPdc3tog over next 3 FPdc, skipping BPdc bet next 3 FPdc, 5 dc in next BPdc; rep from * around to last 6 sts, FPdc3tog, skipping BPdc bet next 3 FPdc, 3 dc in last st, join with sl st in first FPdc3tog—100 sts.

RND 4: Ch 3 (counts as a dc), dc in next 8 sts, *ch 1, skip next st, dc in each of next 9 sts; rep from *around to last st, ch 1, skip last st, join with sl st in first dc—90 dc, 10 ch-1 sps.

RND 5: Ch 2, *FPdecL, dc in ea of next 5 sts, FPdecR, ch 1, dc in ch-1 sp, ch 1; rep from * around, join with sl st in first FpdecL—20 ch-1 sps.

RND 6: Ch 2, *FPdecL, dc in next st, ch 1, skip next dc, dc in next st, FPdecR, ch 1, dc in each of next 3 sts, ch 1; rep from * around, join with sl st in first FpdecL—30 ch-1 sps.

RND 7: Ch 2, *FPdecL, dc in ch-1 sp, FPdecR, ch 1, dc in each of next 5 sts, ch 1; rep from * around, join with sl st in first FPdecL—20 ch-1 sps.

RND 8: Ch 2, FPdc3tog over next 3 sts, ch 1, dc in ea of next 7 sts, ch 1; rep from, * around, join with sl st in first FPdc3tog—20 ch-1 sps.

RND 9: Sl st in first ch-1 sp. Repeat Rnd 4.

RNDS 10–13: Rep Rnds 5–8.

RNDS 14–18: Rep Rnds 9–13.

RNDS 19–20: Rep Rnds 9 and 10.

RND 21: Ch 2, *FPdecL, dc in next dc, ch 1, skip 1 dc, dc in next dc, FPdecR, ch 1, skip ch-1 sp, dc in dc, ch 1, skip ch-1 sp; rep from * around, join with sl st in first FPdecL—30 ch-1 sps.

RND 22: Ch 2, *FPdecL, dc in ch-1 sp, FPdecR, ch 1, dc in dc, ch 1; rep from * around, join with sl st in first FPdecL—20 ch-1 sps.

RND 23: Ch 2, FPdc3tog over next 3 sts, ch 1, dc in next dc, ch 1; rep from, * around, join with sl st in first FPdc3tog—20 ch-1 sps.

RND 24: Ch 3 (counts as dc), dc in ea of next 2 ch-1 sps, *dc in next FPdc3tog, dc in next 2 ch-1sps; rep from * around, join with sl st in beginning ch—30 dc.

RND 25: Ch 3 (counts as dc), sk next dc, *dc in next dc; skip next dc; rep from * around, join with sl st in beginning ch—15 dc.

RND 26: Ch 1 (does not count as a st), [dc2tog over next 2 sts] 7 times, dc in last dc, join with sl st in first dc-2tog—8 dc.

Fasten off, leaving an 8″ (20.5 cm) tail.

Finishing

Weave tail in and out of last rnd of stitches, then pull taut to close hole at top of hat. Weave in the ends.

Lightly spritz with water and pin into shape, let dry.

crocheting *on a budget*

When I'm trying to stick to a budget, I raid my stash first, and I allow myself to buy a new yarn only if it helps me use up at least twice as much stash yarn. For instance, if I only need one ball of new yarn to invigorate the colors I have on hand, and that one ball helps me use three from my stash, that's a great purchase for me. Sometimes adding just a dash of something new can get me excited about yarn that has been sitting around for a while.

✳ *Linda Permann*

tunisian neck lattice

vashti braha

This sleek lightweight triangular scarf, worked side to side from corner to corner, is a refreshing way to experience Tunisian crochet. The featured airy, netlike stitch is warm and cozy when worked in a fine baby alpaca yarn. Best of all, the innovative latticework border uses regular crochet stitches and is crocheted as you go, so there is no additional edging step to complete.

MATERIALS

yarn: Laceweight (#0 Lace).

Shown: Cascade Yarns, Alpaca Lace Paints (100% baby alpaca; 437 yd [400 m]/1.75 oz [50 g]): #9988 (red/brown multi), 1 ball.

hook: J/10 (5.5 mm) 18" (45.5 cm) long Tunisian hook or hook needed to obtain gauge.

notions: 3 stitch markers (optional but recommended); spray bottle with water for blocking; tapestry needle for weaving in ends.

GAUGE

16 sts by 7 rows = 4" × 4" (10 × 10 cm) in Tunisian Knit Single Crochet stitch pattern after blocking. To measure gauge accurately, spritz swatch with water, spread stitches evenly on a flat toweled surface (stitches will expand in height); allow to dry, shake out swatch, then measure it flat.

FINISHED SIZE

50" across widest edge × 22" at deepest center point of triangle (127 × 56 cm).

{notes}

* All increases and decreases are worked steadily along one edge of the scarf while the other edge is worked even throughout.

* Keep a spray bottle filled with water handy as you crochet so that you can periodically mist the rows you've made and see what the finished lacy gauge will look like.

* You will be working the pretty lattice edging as you work each row.

details

Special Stitches

Tunisian Single Crochet (tsc): p. 156.

Tunisian Knit Single Crochet (tksc): p. 156.

Quadruple Treble Crochet (quadtr): Yo (5 times), insert hook in designated st and draw up lp, *yo and draw through 2 lps on hook, rep from * until one lp rem on hook.

Note: When working quadtr, fold the previously made quadtr back and out of your way.

Beginning Increase (beg inc): Ch 1, turn, quadtr in 2 lps of the ch that follows the quadtr of the row below, turn, ch 1 (it's recommended that you place a stitch marker in this ch), tsc in the ch-1 st just before quadtr—inc of 1 st.

Ending Tunisian Single Crochet (endtsc): In the last st of a Fwd pass, insert hook in 2 vertical strands at top of last st of row, yo and pull up lp, ch 1.

Quintuple Treble Crochet (quint-tr): (This stitch is used briefly to improve the deepest point of the triangle.) Yo 6 times, insert hook in designated st and draw up lp, *yo and draw through 2 lps on hook, rep from * until 1 lp rem on hook.

Return Pass Decrease (Retdec): Work RetP until 5 lps rem on hook (1 working lp + stitch marker + 4 lps of row), yo and draw through all 5 lps.

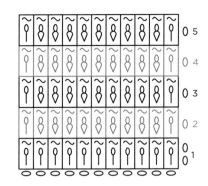

Tunisian Knit Single Crochet Diagram

A. Lattice Increase

Tunisian Knit Single Crochet Stitch Pattern for Gauge Swatch

Refer to **Tunisian Knit Single Crochet** diagram above left for assistance.

Ch 25.

ROW 1 (RS) FWD: Sk first 2 ch (counts as first tsc), (insert hook in next ch, yo and pull up lp, ch 1, leave lp on hook) in ea ch across—24 tsc; 24 lps on hook. **RetP.**

ROW 2 FWD: Ch 1 (counts as first tksc), sk first tsc, tksc in ea tsc across, insert hook in 2 vertical strands at top of last st of row, yo and pull up lp, ch 1 (tsc made)—24 lps on hook. **RetP.**

ROW 3 FWD: Ch 1 (counts as first tksc), sk first tksc, tksc in ea tksc across, insert hook in 2 vertical strands at top of last st of row, yo and pull up lp, ch 1 (tsc made)—24 lps on hook. **RetP.**

Rep Row 3 to desired length.

pattern

Increase Rows

Don't worry about what your stitches look like for the first 5 or 6 rows. The starting corner introduces many new stitches. It will get easier after the initial set-up rows because what you're doing and what the stitches look like will make more sense.

Refer to **Stitch Diagram A** above right for assistance.

INC ROW 1: Make slipknot leaving a 6″ (15 cm) yarn tail and place lp on crochet hook. Ch 5, dtr in 5th ch from hook, ch 1 and place stitch marker in it, turn, tsc in ea of next 2 chs—3 lps on hook. **RetP.**

INC ROW 2: Ch 1, turn, dtr into the center of the body of the dtr, ch 1 and place 2nd marker in it, turn, tsc in first ch—(the one made just before dtr), tksc in first tsc, tksc in next tsc, endtsc in 2 lps of top of end stitch—5 lps on hook. **RetP.**

INC ROW 3: Ch 1, turn, working in front of last dtr made, quadtr in first marked st of the row below, ch 1 and move first marker to ch just made, turn, tsc in first ch-1 made (just before quadtr), tksc in next tsc, tksc in ea tksc across to end, endtsc—7 lps on hook. **RetP.**

NOTE FOR INCREASE ROW 3 AND ALL REM ROWS: When working the quadtr in the marked stitch one row below, push the other tall edge stitches to the back of the work away from you and out of your way.

INC ROW 4: Ch 1, turn, working in front of last quadtr made, quadtr in st with 2nd marker in the row below, ch 1 and move marker to it, turn, tsc in the first ch of the row, tksc in ea tksc across to end, endtsc—9 lps on hook. **RetP.**

INC ROW 5: Ch 1, turn, working in front of last quadtr made, quadtr in marked st one row below, ch 1 and move marker to it, turn, tsc in the first ch of the row, tksc in ea tksc across to end, endtsc—11 lps on hook. **RetP.**

INC ROWS 6–42: Rep Row 5 thirty-seven times—85 tsc.

Do not fasten off. Begin Decrease Rows below.

Decrease Rows

NOTE: Stitches are not decreased until each return pass is completed; therefore do not count loops on hook during the forward pass. (The loops on the hook of the next forward pass will reflect the decreases of the previous row.) During the Forward Pass when you are adding loops onto the hook,

making the most of
your yarn stash

I've tried everything to organize my stash—by weight, color, brand, fiber, surface texture, amount, current vs discontinued. Through process of elimination, I've found that the best method for me is to organize by fiber properties first (how much drape, bounce, stitch-defining sheen, or wintery insulation the yarn will bring to a design, for example), then by weight second. These are the qualities that I decide upon first for a design.

For example: Some alpaca yarns are very wiry, others are fluffy, and stitches behave very differently as a result.

✳ Vashti Braha

you increase 1 stitch. During the Retdec, you decrease 3 stitches; the total number of stitches decreased per row is 2. (This prevents "decrease holes" and matches the drape of the increase rows.)

DEC ROW 1: Ch 1, turn, working in front of last quadtr made, quint-tr in marked st one row below, ch 1 and move marker to it, turn, tsc around first ch made, sk first tsc, tksc in ea st across row to end, endtsc; place 3rd marker for dec after the first 4 lps placed on hook at beg of row. **Retdec.**

DEC ROW 2: Ch 1, turn, working in front of last quint-tr made, quint-tr in marked st one row below as usual, ch 1, turn and move marker to it, tsc around first ch made, sk first dec cluster, tksc in ea st across to end of row, endtsc, move 3rd marker for dec after first 4 lps placed on hook at beg of row. **Retdec.**

NOTE: Placing the 3rd marker is a valuable reminder to decrease at the end of the return pass.

DEC ROW 3: Ch 1, turn, working in front of last quint-tr made, quadtr in marked st one row below as usual, ch 1, turn, tsc around first ch made, sk first dec cluster, tksc in ea st across to end of row, endtsc, place 3rd marker for dec. **Retdec.**

Rep Dec Row 3 until there are no more than 4 lps on hook before beg Retdec. For Retdec, yo and pull through 1 lp on hook, yo and pull through all lps on hook.

FINAL ROW: Ch 1, sc in top of endtsc, ch 7, turn, sc in beg ch 1 of this row, dtr in marked st one row below, ch 2, turn, sl st in ch-7 sp. Fasten off. Weave in ends.

Finishing

For the featured yarn, scarf was thoroughly spritzed with water on both sides then spread out on a flat towel. When blocking, gently and evenly stretch fabric in all directions and arrange border loops so that they hang smoothly and evenly. Allow to air-dry completely.

Vashti Braha has been a full-time professional crochet thinker and tinkerer since 2004. She produces industry-standard crochet patterns, classes, articles, and other materials to promote crochet as an art, hobby, learning tool, and practical medium. Visit her website at designingvashti.com, where you can sign up for her free biweekly crochet newsletter, shop for downloadable crochet patterns, and more.

If you had only one ball of yarn... I crochet shallow triangular scarf/wraps by starting at one side corner, increasing steadily along one edge, and then decreasing steadily when I'm halfway through the ball (I weigh it on a good scale). I use up all of the yarn, and I can pick whatever stitch pattern or technique I like. No matter how big or small this wide triangle comes out, I enjoy wearing it about five different ways.

2–3
balls

botan placemats

marlaina bird

These felted placemats are a perfect project for a housewarming gift or great way to add a little pop of color to your kitchen table. The simple construction coupled with the interesting appliqué makes this a quick and fun project. The set of two placemats uses the entire three balls of yarn, so there will be no waste!

MATERIALS

yarn: Worsted weight (#4 Medium).

Shown: Stitch Nation by Debbie Stoller, Full o' Sheep (100% wool; 155 yd [142 m]/3.5 oz [100 g]): 1 ball each of #2529 Mediterranean (MC); #2925 Passionfruit (A); and #2640 Thyme (B).

hook: I/9 (5.5 mm) or hook needed to obtain gauge.

notions: Tapestry needle for weaving in ends.

GAUGE

16 sts by 9 rows = 4" × 4" (10 × 10 cm) in hdc before felting.

FINISHED SIZE

before felting: 19½" wide × 13½" tall (49.5 × 34.5 cm).

after felting: 16" wide × 12½" tall (40.5 × 31.5 cm).

{note}

* Change color in last yarn over of stitch before new color stitch.

A. Botan Flower Diagram

details

Special Stitch

Shell (sh): (Sc, hdc, 2 dc, hdc, sc) in same sp.

pattern

Botan Flower Motif

Make 1 ea with A and B for CC.

Refer to **Stitch Diagram A** above for assistance.

Ch 6 with MC.

RND 1: 2 sc in 2nd ch from hook and in ea ch across, without twisting rnd, join with a sl st in first sc to form a ring, changing to CC; do not turn—10 sc.

RND 2(RS): With CC, ch 6 (counts as dc and 3 ch), sk next sc, *dc in next sc, ch 3, skip next sc; rep from * 3 times, join with a sl st in 3rd ch of beg ch, do not turn—5 dc and 5 ch-3 sps.

RND 3: Ch 1, sh in each 3-ch sp around, join with a sl st to first sc. Fasten off.

Placemat Body

Make 1 ea with A and B for CC.

Ch 62 with MC (border color).

ROW 1 (RS): Hdc in 3rd ch from hook and in ea ch to end, turn—60 sts.

ROW 2 (WS): Ch 2, hdc in first hdc and in ea hdc across, turn.

ROWS 3–34: Rep Row 2, working in the following color sequence: 3 more rows MC, 24 rows CC, 5 rows MC. Do not fasten off.

Border

RND 1 (RS): With MC, ch 1, *sc in ea hdc across, 3 sc in corner st, rotate to work along the side of placemat, sc evenly along edge to next corner, 3 sc at the corner, rep from * once, join with sl st in first sc. Fasten off.

Finishing

Weave in all loose ends using a tapestry needle. Felt placemat to size (refer to the next section of this pattern, Felting, for assistance and recommendations).

Using MC and tapestry needle, whip-stitch color A motif to corner of color B placemat; whipstitch color B motif to color A placemat. MC whipstitches are decorative.

Felting

It is recommended that you test-felt your yarn. Crochet a swatch using the same yarn in the same colors shown and test-felt it before proceeding with your project.

Felting is irreversible. Please proceed cautiously with the felting process. It is easy to felt "just a little more," but impossible to undo the effects of over-felting.

Place the piece in a pillowcase or zip-pered pillow cover and zip shut or close it with a heavy-duty elastic—this will help to prevent clogging your machine with fibers coming off in the washing process. Place the pillowcase in the washer and add a very small amount of detergent (¼ cap). Set the washer on hot water/cold rinse cycle and the minimum size load. Check the felting process every 1–2 minutes, depending on your machine, detergent, and local water conditions. If using spin cycle to remove excess water, set on lowest set-ting—folds caused by the spin cycle are hard to remove.

After the piece has finished washing, place in the dryer on high heat to fin-ish felting. Check frequently to obtain desired amount of felting. If you have reached the desired level of felting be-fore the piece is dry, remove it from the dryer and allow to dry flat.

As a wife, mother, creative director for Bijou Basin Ranch, knitting and crochet designer, teacher, and host of the Yarn Thing podcast, Marlaina Bird is busy! But she wouldn't change it for anything. You can find more of her designs and listen to her show at MarlyBird.com and thepurseworkshop.com.

If you had only one ball of yarn . . .
My favorite thing to make with a ball of yarn is a cowl. Not only are they very useful, but they are stylish as well.

tapestry basket

carol ventura

If you like to crochet loosely, this project is for you because it's tapestry crocheted with a large hook and loose stitches. Two colors are carried from beginning to end to produce a substantial fabric. Then, the basket shrinks and felts like magic in a washing machine. The beauty of felted tapestry crochet is that the pattern is visible on the inside and the outside.

{notes}

* This piece is worked as a spiral, so do not join. To keep track of where each round ends, slip a stitch marker into the top of the last st of the round.

* Only two yarns are tapestry crocheted in each round, so carry the third color not being worked, but place it to the side to keep it from tangling.

* The motif is ten stitches wide and there are ten increases per round. Therefore, smaller baskets could be made following the same instructions by beginning the sides in an earlier round at desired diameter and by crocheting fewer repeats for desired depth.

MATERIALS

yarn: Worsted weight (#4 Medium).

Shown: Cascade Yarns, Cascade 220 Wool, (100% Peruvian highland wool; 220 yd [200 m] /3.5 oz [110 g]): 1 ball ea of #7814 chartreuse (MC); #8412 pear (CC1); #9475 sage (CC2).

hook: K/10.5 (6.5 mm) or hook needed to obtain gauge.

notions: Tapestry needle for weaving in ends; stitch markers; liquid dishwashing soap (see Finishing on p. 55).

GAUGE

12 sc by 12 rows = 4" × 4" (10 × 10 cm).

FINISHED SIZE

before felting: 21" wide × 18" high (53.5 × 46 cm).

after felting: 8" diameter × 11" high (20.5 × 28 cm).

details

Special Instructions: Tapestry Crochet

To carry nonworking yarn color: Lay nonworking yarn color over top of sts being worked, then sc across as usual with color indicated, inserting the hook into the next stitch and completing the sc around the nonworking yarn, encasing it between sts. If done correctly, it will not be visible from front or back of work.

To change color: Work stitch until 2 lps remain on hook, drop working yarn color, pick up nonworking (carried) yarn color and draw through both lps on hook.

pattern

Base

Starting at center, with MC, leaving 6" (15 cm) tail, ch 4; join with sl st to form a ring.

RND 1: Work 5 sc in ring (while working over the tail)—5 sc.

RND 2: Cont to carry tail and beg to carry CC1. With MC, 2 sc in ea sc around—10 sc.

RND 3: Cut MC tail and beg carrying CC2. With MC, carrying CC1 and CC2, 2 sc in ea sc around—20 sc.

RND 4: With MC, carrying CC1 and CC2, [2 sc in next sc, sc in next sc] 10 times—30 sc.

RND 5: With MC, carrying CC1 and CC2, [2 sc in next sc, sc in next 2 sc] 10 times—40 sc.

RND 6: With MC, carrying CC1 and CC2, [2 sc in next sc, sc in next 3 sc] 10 times—50 sc.

RND 7: With MC, carrying CC1 and CC2, [2 sc in next sc, sc in next 4 sc] 10 times—60 sc.

RND 8: With MC, carrying CC1 and CC2, [2 sc in next sc, sc in next 5 sc] 10 times—70 sc.

RND 9: With MC, carrying CC1 and CC2, [2 sc in next sc, sc in next 6 sc] 10 times—80 sc.

RND 10: With MC, carrying CC1 and CC2, [2 sc in next sc, sc in next 7 sc] 10 times—90 sc.

RND 11: With MC, carrying CC1 and CC2, [2 sc in next sc, sc in next 8 sc] 10 times—100 sc.

RND 12: With MC, carrying CC1 and CC2, [2 sc in next sc, sc in next 9 sc] 10 times—110 sc.

RND 13: With MC, carrying CC1 and CC2, [2 sc in next sc, sc in next 10 sc] 10 times—120 sc.

RND 14: With MC, carrying CC1 and CC2, [2 sc in next sc, sc in next 11 sc] 10 times—130 sc.

Sides

See the **Colorwork Diagram** below to change colors.

RND 1: Tapestry crochet [3 MC, 4 CC1, 3 MC] 13 times—130 sc.

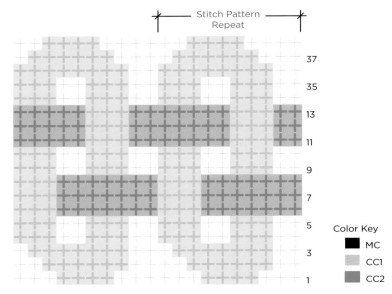

Colorwork Diagram

Color Key
- MC
- CC1
- CC2

RND 2: Tapestry crochet [2 MC, 6 CC1, 2 MC] 13 times—130 sc.

RND 3: Tapestry crochet [2 MC, 7 CC1, 1 MC] 13 times—130 sc.

RNDS 4–5: Tapestry crochet [2 MC, 3 CC1] 26 times—130 sc.

RNDS 6–8: Tapestry crochet [7 CC2, 3 CC1] 13 times—130 sc.

RNDS 9–10: Tapestry crochet [2 MC, 3 CC1] 26 times—130 sc.

RNDS 11–13: Tapestry crochet [2 CC2, 3 CC1, 5 CC2] 13 times—130 sc.

Rep Rnds 4–13 three times.

RNDS 44–45: Tapestry crochet [2 MC, 3 CC1] 26 times—130 sc.

RND 46: Tapestry crochet [2 MC, 8 CC1] 13 times—130 sc.

RND 47: Tapestry crochet [3 MC, 6 CC1, 1 MC] 13 times—130 sc.

RND 48: Tapestry crochet [4 MC, 4 CC1, 2 MC] 13 times—130 sc.

RND 49: With MC, carrying CC1 and CC2, sc in ea sc around—130 sc.

Cut the carried CC1 and CC2, with MC, sl st in next sc. Cut MC, leaving a 6″ (15 cm) tail, then yo and pull it through the lp on the hook. Weave in end through sts in last rnd.

Finishing

Wash the basket twice in a washing machine (set to hot wash and cold rinse) with 4 tablespoons of liquid dishwashing soap and rinse it twice after the last wash to felt it. Let it dry, then block it with a steam iron. Then, if you prefer the look of the inside better than the outside, turn the basket inside out (this was done to the sample basket so that the "wrong" side is featured on the exterior of the basket).

making the most of
your yarn stash

To use up small balls of leftover yarn, try using a different color for each of the horizontal stripes in the Tapestry Basket, creating a fun, colorful effect. You'll just need to make sure that all of the yarn you use is feltable.

✳ *Carol Ventura*

Colorful shoulder bags from Guatemala initially inspired **Carol Ventura** to give tapestry crochet a try in the 1970s. More than thirty years later, she's still excited about its design potential. For more about Carol's tapestry crochet books and videos, please visit tapestrycrochet .com/blog and tapestrycrochet.com.

If you had only one ball of yarn… I would honestly need two balls in contrasting colors. Recently, I've been crocheting hats, experimenting with motifs and styles.

blooming beauty purse

tracie barrett

This purse works up quickly either for a last-minute gift or for putting the finishing touch on that perfect outfit. The lining is made using fat quarters (precut fabric remnants), so feel free to go bold without spending a lot of money. The fabric lining prevents the bag from stretching out—toss in all your essentials and go!

MATERIALS

yarn: DK weight (#3 Light).

Shown: Filatura Di Crosa, Zara (100% extrafine merino superwash; 136.5 yd [125 m]/1.75 oz [50 g]): #1396 off white (MC), 1 ball; #1894 fawn (CC1), 1 ball; #1896 taupe (CC2), 1 ball.

hook: F/5 (3.75mm) or hook needed to obtain gauge.

notions: Tapestry needle for weaving in ends; 2 fat quarters (18" × 21" [45.5 × 53.5 cm]); sewing needle and matching thread; 2 purse handles (circular, D-shaped, or similar; handles shown are 6½" [16.5 cm] across from end to end).

GAUGE

1 finished motif (3 rounds) = 4¼" (11 cm) from point to point.

FINISHED SIZE

15" across × 9½" deep (38 × 24 cm; not including handles).

{note}
---

* Work two rounds of motifs, then third round is worked to join motifs together. Follow joining diagram to join motifs together.

details

Special Stitches

2 Treble Crochet Cluster (2tr-cl): [Yo twice, insert hook into next sp, yo, draw up a lp [yo, draw through 2 lps) twice] twice in same sp, yo, pull through all 3 lps on hook.

3 Double Crochet Cluster (3dc-cl): p. 155.

4 Double Crochet Cluster (4dc-cl): p. 155.

pattern

Blooming Motif

Make 1, Join 17.

MOTIF A: Make 9 motifs using MC for Rnd 1, CC1 for Rnd 2, and CC2 for Rnd 3.

MOTIF B: Make 9 motifs using CC1 for Rnd 1, MC for Rnd 2, and CC2 for Rnd 3.

See **Stitch Diagram A** at right for assistance.

Ch 9, sl st to form ring.

RND 1 (RS): Ch 3, tr in ring (counts as tr-cl), ch 2, [2tr-cl, ch 2] 11 times in ring, sl st in top of first tr. Fasten off—12 tr-cl.

RND 2: With RS facing, join yarn in any ch-2 sp, ch 2, work 3dc-cl in same ch-2 sp, ch 5, (4dc-cl, ch 5) in each ch-2 sp around, sl st in top of first 3dc-cl. Fasten off—12 dc-cl.

RND 3: With RS facing, join yarn with sc in any ch-5 sp, *ch 7, sl st in 4th ch from hook (picot made), ch 3, sc in next ch-5

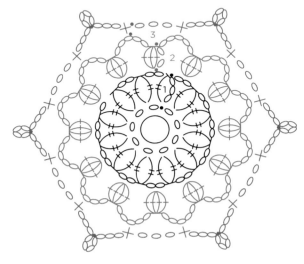

A. Blooming Motif

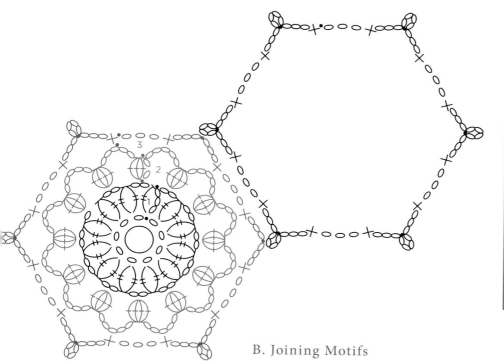

B. Joining Motifs

sp, ch 3, sc in next ch-5 sp; rep from * around, omitting last sc, join with sl st to first sc. Fasten off.

Joining

Join motifs using CC2 and **Stitch Diagram B** above and Motif Layout on p. 61. Join motifs in order listed. After joining Motifs 1–14, fold purse in half to join last 4 motifs.

JOINING MOTIFS 1–4, 5, AND 10: Join yarn with sc in any ch-5 sp, [ch 7, sl st in 4th ch from hook (picot made), ch 3, sc in next sp, ch 3, sc in next sp] 4 times, [ch 3, sl st into adjoining picot, ch 3, sc in next sp, ch 3, sc in next sp] twice, omitting last sc, join with sl st in first sc. Fasten off.

JOINING MOTIFS 6–8, 11–13: Cont with directions above, joining 3 sides by replacing picots with a sl st to the adjoining picot.

JOINING MOTIFS 9 AND 14: Cont with directions above, joining 2 sides by replacing picots with a sl st to the adjoining picot.

JOINING MOTIFS 15–18: Cont with directions above, joining all the sides by replacing picots with a sl st to the adjoining picot.

finishing

Lining

Place the 2 fat quarters right sides facing, then fold in half widthwise. Place the purse on top of the fabric, with the bottom of the purse sitting against the fold. Trace outline of purse onto fabric, adding ½" (1.3 cm) seam allowances on each side and at the top edge. On each fabric, mark the spots at each side, near the top, where the motif join ends. Cut the shape from the fabrics and then separate the 2 pieces. Fold each piece in half, right sides facing, along the existing crease. Sew each side with ½"

(1.3 cm) seams, stitching only to the marks and leaving the top edges open. Turn one bag right side out and then press the top edge and unsewn side edges of each bag ½" (1.3 cm) toward the wrong side. Insert the bag that is wrong side out into the other bag so that wrong sides are facing and pin together along the open edges. Topstitch around the top edge of the bag (pivoting to topstitch along the side vents as well), about ⅛" (3 mm) from the top edge. Insert the completed lining purse into the crochet purse and use a sewing needle and thread to whipstitch the lining into the purse, around the top edge.

Handles

Attach handles as desired. Handles shown were attached in following manner (this will vary depending on handles chosen): Join CC into picot with sc, *(sc around handle, sc in next st) rep from * to end of opening. Fasten off and weave in ends.

Tracie Barrett is a crochet designer living in sunny Florida. For more great designs, head to fibersbytracie.com. You can also find her on Ravelry.com and on Twitter as TracieCrochets.

If you had only one ball of yarn... I usually make some sort of accessory. I love cowls because here in Florida, they're much easier to wear than scarves.

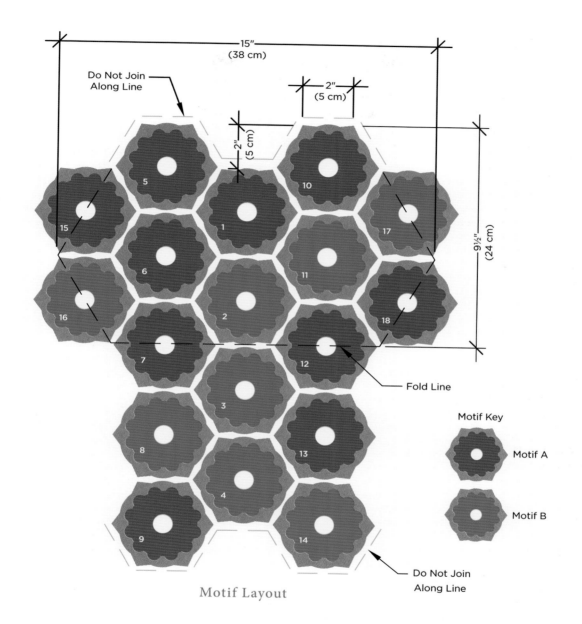

15"
(38 cm)

Do Not Join
Along Line

2"
(5 cm)

2"
(5 cm)

5

10

15

1

17

6

11

7

12

16

18

2

Fold Line

Motif Key

3

Motif A

13

8

Motif B

4

9

14

9½"
(24 cm)

Motif Layout

Do Not Join
Along Line

nedburt sock puppet

robyn chachula

If you have a few small balls of yarn and no idea what to do with them, Nedburt is your puppet. His quirky smile will charm kids of all ages (and adults, too). Make up a set of two or three in bright colors for a fun and interactive gift for the young children in your life.

MATERIALS

yarn: DK weight (#3 Light).

Shown: Red Heart, Designer Sport (100% acrylic; 279 yd [255 m]/3 oz [85 g]): 1 ball each of #3801 aqua ice (A); #3650 pistachio (B); #3261 terra cotta (C).

hook: G/7 (4.5 mm) or hook needed to obtain gauge.

notions: Tapestry needle for weaving in ends; two ⅝" (15 mm) buttons.

GAUGE

16 sts by 14 rows = 4″ × 4¼″ (10 × 11 cm) alternating rows of sc and dc.

FINISHED SIZE

9½" circumference × 11" long (24 × 28 cm).

{notes}

* Three balls are enough for nearly six sock puppets, two in each color combination, which makes this project perfect for odds and ends in your stash.

* Color combination 1: Use A as MC; B as CC1 and C as CC2.

* Color combination 2: Use B as MC; C as CC1; and A as CC2.

* Color combination 3: Use C as MC; A as CC1; and B as CC2.

pattern

Head

Refer to **Stitch Diagram A** at right for assistance.

Ch 9 with MC.

RND 1 (WS): Sc in 2nd ch from hook and in ea of next 6 ch sts, 3 sc in last ch, turn work 180 degrees, (work in free lps of chs), sc in ea of next 6 ch sts, 2 sc in next ch, sl st in first sc, turn—18 sc.

RND 2: Ch 3 (counts as dc), 3 dc in first sc, dc in next 8 sc, 3 dc in next sc, dc in ea of the rem sc, sl st in top of tch, turn—22 dc.

RND 3: Ch 1, sc bet tch and next dc, sc bet the next 7 dc, [2 sc between the next 2 dc] twice, sc between the next 9 dc, [2 sc bet the next 2 dc] twice, sc bet the last dc and tch, sl st in first sc, turn—26 sc.

RND 4: Ch 3 (counts as dc), dc in next 2 sc, 2 dc in ea of next 2 dc, dc in next 11 sc, 2 dc in next 2 dc, dc in ea of the rem sc around, sl st in top of tch, turn—30 dc.

RND 5: Ch 1, sc bet ea st around, sl st in first sc, turn—30 sc.

RND 6: Ch 3 (counts as dc), dc in ea sc around, sl st in top of tch, turn.

Rep Rnds 5–6 five times. Fasten off, weave in ends.

Tongue

Ch 7 with MC.

RND 1 (WS): Sc in 2nd ch from hook and in ea ch to last ch, 3 sc in last ch, turn work 180 degrees, (work in free lps of chs), sc in ea ch across to first sc, 2 sc in next ch, sl st to first sc, turn—14 sc.

RND 2: Ch 3 (counts as dc), 3 dc in next sc, dc in next 6 sc, 3 dc in next sc, dc in ea of the rem sc, sl st to top of tch, turn—18 dc.

RND 3: Ch 1, sc bet tch and next dc, sc bet the next 5 dc, [2 sc bet the next 2 dc] twice, sc bet the next 7 dc, [2 sc bet the next 2 dc] twice, sc bet the last dc and tch, sl st to first sc, turn—22 sc.

RND 4: Ch 3 (counts as dc), dc in next 2 sc, 2 dc in next 2 dc, dc in next 9 sc, 2 dc in next 2 dc, dc in ea of the rem sc around, sl st to top of tch, turn— 26 dc.

RND 5: Ch 1, sc bet ea st around, sl st in first sc, turn—26 sc.

RND 6: Ch 3 (counts as dc), dc in ea sc around, sl st in top of tch, turn.

Rep Rnds 5–6 three times, fasten off.

Body

Flatten Tongue and Head and center Tongue on Head, lining up the sts across one side, pin together. Locate center of matched sides, join MC in 5th st to the left of center st.

JOINING ROW: Ch 1, working through double thickness, sc in first st, sc in next 10 sc.

RND 1: Sc bet ea dc around Tongue, then sc bet ea dc around Head, sl st in first sc on Tonue to join, turn—36 sc around Body.

RND 2: Ch 3 (counts as dc), dc in ea sc around, sl st in top of tch, turn.

RND 3: Ch 1, sc bet ea st around, sl st in first sc, turn.

Rep Rnds 2–3 six more times, Rep Rnd 2 once do not turn, fasten off MC.

RND 17: Join CC2, ch 1, sc between ea st around, sl st to first sc, fasten off CC2, do not turn.

RND 18: Join CC1, ch 3 (counts as dc), dc in ea sc around, sl st in top of tch, fasten off CC1, do not turn.

RND 19: Join CC2, ch 1, sc bet ea st around, sl st in first sc, fasten off CC2, do not turn.

RND 20: Join MC, ch 3 (counts as dc), dc in ea sc around, sl st in top of tch, turn.

RND 21: Ch 1, sc bet ea st around, sl st in first sc, turn.

RND 22: Sl st in ea sc around, fasten off, weave in ends.

Eyes

Make 2.

Make an adjustable ring with MC.

RND 1: Ch 1, 4 sc in ring, tighten ring, do not join or turn—4 sc.

RND 2: 2 sc in ea sc around, do not join or turn—8 sc.

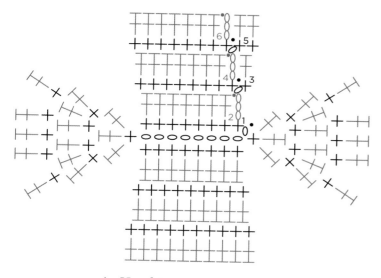

A. Head Increase Diagram

RND 3: *Sc in next sc, 2 sc in next sc, rep from * around, do not join or turn—12 sc.

RNDS 4–5: Sc in ea sc around, do not join or turn.

RND 6: *Sc2tog over next 2 sc, sc in next sc, rep from * around, do not join or turn—8 sc.

RND 7: Sc2tog over next 2 sc around, fasten off, weave end through rem sts to close—4 sc. Fasten off, leaving a long tail for sewing.

Flatten Eye and sew button to center of Eye. Using the photo on page 62 as a guide, sew Eyes to Rnd 10 of Head with tapestry needle and yarn tail.

Ears

Make 2.

Make an adjustable ring with CC2.

RND 1: Ch 1, 4 sc in ring, tighten ring, do not join or turn—4 sc.

RND 2: 2 sc in ea sc around, do not join or turn—8 sc.

RNDS 3–4: Sc in ea sc around, do not join or turn.

RND 5: Sc2tog over next 2 sc around, sl st to first sc—4 sc.

Stem

ROW 6: Ch 6, sc in 2nd ch from hook and in ea ch across, sl st in next sc in Rnd 5, turn work 180 degrees, sc in free lps of each ch across, turn—10 sc.

ROW 7: Pinch Row 6 together so sc line up, sl st through both sc at once up stem, sl st to Rnd 5, fasten off, leave long tail for sewing.

Pinch top of Ear flat, sew through center to secure. Sew Ears to Head, with ends of stems 3 rnds above Eyes, about 1" (2.5 cm) apart.

Finishing

With CC2, use a satin stitch to create a nose on the Head at Rnd 6 around 2 dc posts at once to desired thickness. Cut twenty-eight 3" (7.5 cm) lengths of CC1. Holding 2 strands together, fold in half. Insert hook around post (from front to back to front) of one of the 7 center dc on the head one round above ears. Place folded strands on hook and pull lp through stitch. Pull ends through lp and tighten (knotting the stands to the post of the dc). Rep on all 7 center dc for hair of puppet. Trim hair to about ¾" (2 cm) in length.

natalie shrug

megan granholm

This 1950s-inspired shrug is a quick project with lots of feminine appeal. Though it is crocheted in traditionally unforgiving Tunisian stitches, the stitch pattern allows for plenty of stretch. Pair it with a sundress or a tank top and jeans for just a little shoulder cover and a lot of style.

MATERIALS

yarn: Fingering weight (#1 Super Fine).

Shown: Filatura di Crosa, Zarina (100% extrafine Merino wool; 181 yd [165 m]/1.75 oz [50 g]): #1754 plum, 2 (2, 3, 3, 3, 3) balls.

hook: F/5 (3.75mm) Tunisian hook or hook needed to obtain gauge.

notions: Tapestry needle for weaving in ends; spray bottle with water and straight pins for blocking.

GAUGE

23 sts by 16 rows = 4″ × 4″ (10 × 10 cm) in stitch pattern.

FINISHED SIZE

XS (S, M, L, XL, 2XL) shrug is sized to fit 32 (34, 36, 38, 40, 42)″ (81.5 [86.5, 96.5, 101.5, 106.5] cm) bust with a close fit. Sample shown is a size S (32½″ [82.5 cm] bust).

finished chest: 32½ (34½, 37½, 39, 41, 43)″ (82.5 [87.5, 95, 99, 104, 109] cm).

finished length: 7 (7, 7½, 8, 8½, 8½)″ (18 [18, 19, 20.5, 21.5, 21.5] cm).

{notes}

* The first loop on hook counts as a stitch in all stitch counts.

* Work the last st of each row in two vertical strands at top of last st.

* When decreasing, be sure that the 2tog stitch follows the stitch pattern. For example, if decreasing at the beginning of a row and the next stitch to be worked is a tps, work tdc2tog to decrease; if the next stitch to be worked is a tps, work tps2tog to decrease.

schematics

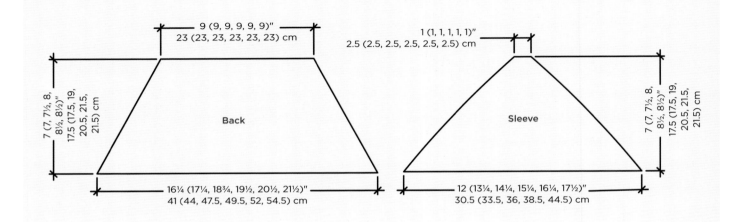

details

Special Stitches

Tunisian Simple Stitch (tss): p. 156.

Tunisian Double Crochet (tdc): p. 156.

Tunisian Purl Stitch (tps): With yarn in front of work, insert into next vertical bar as for tss, yo, draw yarn through st.

Tunisian Griddle Stitch Pattern (tgsp)

See the **Tunisian Griddle Stitch Pattern** diagram on page 69 for assistance.

Ch 24.

ROW 1: Tss in 2nd ch from hook and in ea ch across. **RetP**—24 sts.

ROW 2: Tdc in 2nd st from hook, (tps in next st, tdc in next st) across to last st,

tss in 2 vertical strands at top of last st. **RetP.**

ROW 3: (Tps in tdc from prev row, tdc in tps from prev row) across to last st, tss in 2 vertical strands at top of last st. **RetP.**

Rep Row 3 of stitch pattern.

pattern

Back

Refer to **Stitch Diagram A** on page 69 for assistance.

Ch 94 (100, 108, 112, 118, 124).

ROW 1 (RS): Tss in 2nd ch from hook and in ea ch across. **RetP**—94 (100, 108, 112, 118, 124) sts.

XS (S, M, L) ONLY:

ROW 2: Work Row 2 of tgsp across.

XL (2XL) ONLY:

ROW 2: Tdc2tog over 2nd and 3rd st (dec made), cont in tgsp across to last 3 sts, tps2tog over next 2 sts, tss in 2 vertical strands at top of last st. **RetP**—116 (122) sts.

ALL SIZES:

ROW 3: Tdc2tog over 2nd and 3rd st (dec made), cont in tgsp across to last 3 sts, tps2tog over next 2 sts, tss in 2 vertical strands at top of last st. **RetP**—92 (98, 106, 110, 116, 122) sts.

ROWS 4-6: Rep Row 3—86 (92, 100, 104, 108, 114) sts.

XS ONLY:

ROW 7: Cont in tgsp across.

S (M, L, XL, 2XL) ONLY:

ROW 7: Rep Row 3—90 (98, 102, 106, 112) sts.

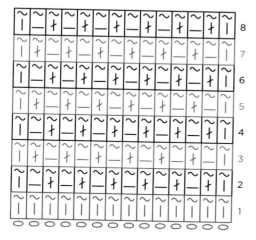

Tunisian Griddle Stitch Pattern Diagram

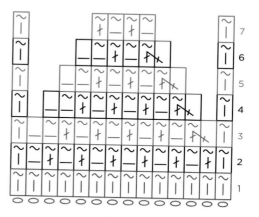

A. Body Decrease

ALL SIZES:

ROWS 8-11: Rep Row 3—78 (82, 90, 94, 98, 102) sts.

XS (S) ONLY:

ROW 12: Cont in tgsp across.

M (L, XL) ONLY:

ROW 12: Rep Row 3—88 (92, 96) sts.

2XL ONLY:

ROW 12: Tdc2tog over 2nd and 3rd st, tdc2tog over next 2 sts, cont in patt across to last 5 sts, [tps2tog over next 2 sts] twice, tss in 2 vertical strands at top of last st. **RetP**—100 sts.

ALL SIZES:

ROWS 13-16: Rep Row 3—70 (74, 80, 84, 88, 92) sts.

XS ONLY:

ROW 17: Cont in tgsp across.

S (M, L, XL) ONLY:

ROW 17: Rep Row 3—72 (78, 82, 86) sts.

2XL ONLY:

ROW 17: Rep Row 12—88 sts.

ALL SIZES:

ROWS 18-21: Rep Row 3—62 (64, 70, 74, 78, 80) sts.

XS (S) ONLY:

ROW 22: Cont in tgsp across.

M (L, XL) ONLY:

ROW 22: Rep Row 3—68 (72, 76) sts.

2XL ONLY:

Rep Row 12—76 sts.

ALL SIZES:

ROWS 23-27: Rep Row 3—52 (54, 58, 62, 66, 66) sts.

Rep Row 3 one (three, five, seven, seven) time(s). Fasten off.

Sleeves (make 2)

Ch 70 (76, 82, 88, 94, 100).

ALL SIZES:

ROW 1: Tss across—70 (76, 82, 88, 94, 100) sts.

XS (S, M, L, XL) ONLY:

ROW 2: Tdc2tog over 2nd and 3rd st (dec made), cont in tgsp across to last 3 sts, tps2tog over next 2 sts, tss in 2 vertical strands at top of last st. **RetP**—68 (74, 80, 86, 92) sts.

Megan Granholm's style of clean, classic garments with a design twist has been featured in *Interweave Crochet* and *Inside Crochet*, on crochetme.com, and in several books. Megan lives, works, and plays in Corvallis, Oregon. Find her on Ravelry.com or at her blog, loopdedoo.blogspot.com.

If you had only one ball of yarn…
Special yarns usually sit on my desk for a very long time because I must first stare at them and fondle them. It's part of my design process. But I usually end up making a scarf or cowl so that it can be the star of an outfit.

2XL ONLY:
ROW 2: Cont in tgsp across.

ALL SIZES:
ROW 3: Tdc2tog over 2nd and 3rd st (dec made), cont in tgsp across to last 3 sts, tps2tog over next 2 sts, tss in 2 vertical strands at top of last st. **RetP**—67 (72, 78, 84, 90, 98) sts.

XS (S, 2XL) ONLY:
ROW 4: Rep Row 3—64 (70, 96) sts.

M, (L, XL) ONLY:
ROW 4: Tdc2tog over 2nd and 3rd st, tdc2tog over next 2 sts, cont in patt across to last 5 sts, [tps2tog over next 2 sts] twice, tss in 2 vertical strands at top of last st. **RetP**—74 (80, 86) sts.

ALL SIZES:
ROWS 5-6: Rep Rows 3-59—66 (70, 76, 82, 92) sts.

ROW 7: Tps2tog, tdc2tog, work in patt across to last 5 sts, dec twice, tss in last st—56 (62, 66, 72, 78, 88) sts.

XS (S, M, L, XL) ONLY:
ROW 8: Rep Row 3—54 (60, 64, 70, 76) sts.

2XL ONLY:
ROW 8: Rep Row 7—84 sts.

ALL SIZES:
ROW 9: Rep Row 3—52 (58, 62, 68, 74, 82) sts.

ROW 10: Rep Row 7—48 (54, 58, 64, 70, 78) sts.

ROWS 11-12: Rep Row 3—44 (50, 54, 60, 66, 74) sts.

XS ONLY:
ROW 13: Rep Row 3—42 sts.

S (M, L, XL, 2XL) ONLY:
ROW 13: Rep Row 7—46 (50, 56, 62, 70) sts.

XS (S, M, L, XL) ONLY:
ROW 14: Rep Row 3—40 (44, 48, 54, 60) sts.

2XL ONLY:
ROW 14: Rep Row 7—66 sts.

ALL SIZES:
ROWS 15-18: Rep Rows 9-12—30 (34, 38, 44, 50, 56) sts.

XS ONLY:
ROW 19: Rep Row 3—28 sts.

S (M, L, XL, 2XL) ONLY:
ROW 19: Rep Row 7—30 (34, 40, 46, 52) sts.

XS (S, M, L, XL) ONLY:
ROW 20: Rep Row 3—26 (28, 32, 38, 44) sts.

2XL ONLY:
ROW 20: Rep Row 7—48 sts.

ALL SIZES:
ROWS 21-24: Rep Rows 9-12—16 (18, 22, 28, 34, 38) sts.

ROW 25: Rep Row 7—12 (14, 18, 24, 30, 34) sts.

XS (S, M, L, XL) ONLY:
ROW 26: Rep Row 3—10 (12, 16, 22, 28, 30) sts.

2XL ONLY:
ROW 26: Rep Row 7—30 sts.

Sleeve Ribbing

Turn Sleeve upside-down, attach yarn to first foundation ch; ch 6.

ROW 1: Sc in 2nd ch from hook and across—6 sc. Sl st to ea of next 2 foundation ch, turn.

ROW 2: Sc blp across. Ch 1, turn.

ROW 3: Sc blp across, sl st to ea of next 2 foundation ch, turn.

Rep Rows 2–3 for ribbed pattern, ending with Row 2 of patt.

After working last row, fasten off, leaving a long tail for sewing.

Finishing

Blocking and Seaming

Pin Back and Sleeves to finished measurements (see Schematics on page 68). Spritz with water and allow to dry. Whipstitch Sleeves to Back. Using yarn tail and working through front lps of sts, whipstitch last row of ribbing to foundation ch.

Edging

With RS facing, join yarn to edge of shrug with a sl st. Sk 2 sts, 2 tr in next st, sl st to 4th row above edge of shrug, 2 tr in same st as prev 2 tr, sk 2 sts, sl st in next st. Rep evenly around to end, finishing with sl st in same st as joining. Fasten off, weave in ends.

ALL SIZES:

ROW 27: Rep Row 3—8 (10, 14, 20, 26, 28) sts.

XS ONLY:

ROW 28: Rep Row 3—6 sts. Fasten off.

S ONLY:

ROW 28: Rep Row 7—6 sts. Fasten off.

M (L, XL, 2XL) ONLY:

ROW 28: Rep Row 7—8 (16, 22, 24) sts.

ROWS 29–30: Rep Row 3—6 (12, 18, 20) sts.

M ONLY:

Fasten off.

L (XL, 2XL) ONLY:

ROW 31: Rep Row 7—8 (14, 16) sts.

L ONLY:

ROW 32: Rep Row 3—6 sts. Fasten off.

XL ONLY:

ROW 32: Rep Row 3—12 sts.

2XL ONLY:

ROW 32: Rep Row 7—12 sts.

XL (2XL) ONLY:

ROW 33: Rep Row 3—10 (10) sts.

ROW 34: Rep Row 7—6 (6) sts. Fasten off.

giselle vest

simona merchant-dest

This simple lacy top is a versatile addition to your wardrobe. Wear it alone as a summer top with a simple skirt or layer it over a blouse and slacks to add a sweet feminine touch to a work outfit. The top creates a pleasant slimming effect with vertical striping and a pretty lace panel at the center front to draw the eye, making this a great gift for a friend or for you!

MATERIALS

yarn: Sock weight (#1 Super Fine).

Shown: Cascade Yarns, Heritage (75% merino superwash, 25% nylon; 437 yd [400 m]/3.5 oz [100 g]): #5648 strawberry cream (MC), 2 (2, 3, 3, 3, 3) balls.

hook: D/3 (3.25 mm) or hook needed to obtain gauge.

notions: Spray bottle with water and straight pins for blocking; tapestry needle for weaving in ends; 2 removable markers.

GAUGE

28 sts by 12 rows = 4" × 4" (10 × 10 cm) in Flower and Stripe Stitch Pattern.

28 sts by 10 rows = 4" × 3" (10 × 7.5 cm) in Center Stitch Pattern.

FINISHED SIZE

S (M, L, XL, 2XL, 3XL) is sized to fit a 32 (36, 40, 44, 48, 52)" (81.5 [91.5, 101.5, 112, 114.5, 132] cm) bust. Top shown is a size M.

finished chest: 32 (36, 40, 44, 48, 52)" (81.5 [91.5, 101.5, 112, 114.5, 132] cm).

finished length: 17½ (18, 18½, 19, 19½, 20)" (44.5 [45.5, 47, 48.5, 49.5, 51] cm).

{note}

* Body is worked in one piece sideways, then it is seamed together at center back. All edges are worked in rows back and forth, joined in rounds. Shoulder straps are worked separately and seamed to body.

schematic

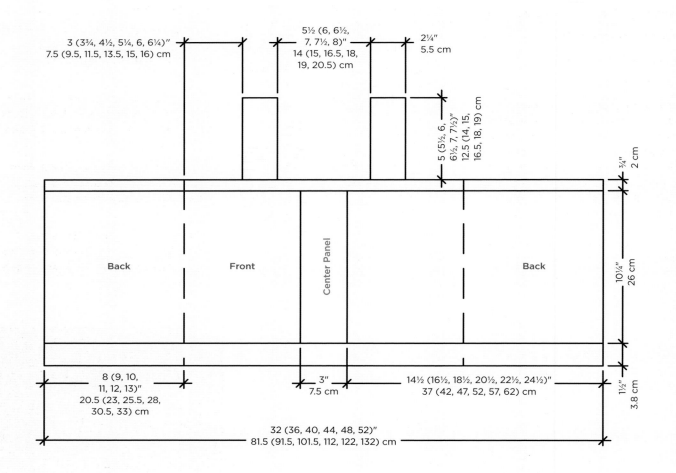

3 (3¾, 4½, 5¼, 6, 6¼)"
7.5 (9.5, 11.5, 13.5, 15, 16) cm

5½ (6, 6½,
7, 7½, 8)"
14 (15, 16.5, 18,
19, 20.5) cm

2¼"
5.5 cm

5 (5½, 6,
6½, 7, 7½)"
12.5 (14, 15,
16.5, 18, 19) cm

¾"
2 cm

Back

Front

Center Panel

Back

10¼"
26 cm

8 (9, 10,
11, 12, 13)"
20.5 (23, 25.5, 28,
30.5, 33) cm

3"
7.5 cm

14½ (16½, 18½, 20½, 22½, 24½)"
37 (42, 47, 52, 57, 62) cm

1½"
3.8 cm

32 (36, 40, 44, 48, 52)"
81.5 (91.5, 101.5, 112, 122, 132) cm

details

Special Stitches

Foundation Single Crochet (fsc): p. 154.

2-Hdc Cluster (2hdc-cl): p. 154.

2-Dc Cluster (2dc-cl): p. 155.

4-Dc Cluster (4dc-cl): p. 155.

5-Dc Cluster (5dc-cl): (Yo, insert hook in last dc worked, yo, draw yarn through st, yo, draw yarn through 2 lps on hook) twice in same st, sk next 2 sts, yo, insert hook in next dc, yo, draw yarn through st, yo, draw yarn through 2 lps on hook, sk next 2 sts, (insert hook in next dc, yo, draw yarn through st, yo, draw yarn through 2 lps on hook) twice in same st, yo, draw yarn through 6 lps on hook.

2-Dc-1tr Cluster (2dc-1tr-cl): (Yo, insert hook in indicated st, yo, draw yarn through st, yo, draw yarn through 2 lps on hook) twice in same st, sk next 5dc-cl and ch-3 sp, yo twice, insert hook in last sc, draw yarn through st, (yo, draw yarn through 2 lps on hook) twice, yo, draw yarn through 4 lps on hook.

Stitch Pattern

Flower and Stripe Stitch Pattern (fssp)

(Multiple of 6 sts plus 1)

See **Flower and Stripe Stitch Pattern** diagram below for assistance.

FOUNDATION ROW: 31 fsc, turn.

ROW 1 (RS): Ch 3 (count as dc), dc in ea st across, turn.

ROW 2: Ch 4 (count as dc, ch 1), sk first 2 dc, *dc in next dc, ch 1, sk next dc; rep from * across to tch, dc in top of tch, turn.

ROW 3: Ch 3 (count as dc), *dc in next ch-1 sp, dc in next dc; rep from * across to tch, dc in ch-1 sp of tch, dc in 3rd ch of tch, turn.

ROW 4: Ch 1, sc in first dc, *ch 3, starting in first st, 5dc-cl over next 7 sts, ch 4, sc in last dc worked; rep from * across, turn.

ROW 5: Ch 4 (counts as tr), sk next 3 ch sts, 2dc-cl in next ch of ch-4 sp, *ch 4, sc in last ch worked, ch 3, starting in

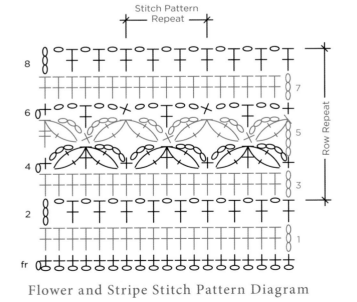

Flower and Stripe Stitch Pattern Diagram

same st, work 4dc-cl, rep from * across to last 5dc-cl, ch 4, sc in same ch of ch-4, ch 3, starting in same ch, work 2dc-1tr-cl, ending in last sc, turn.

ROW 6: Ch 1, sc in first st, *ch 2, sk next ch-3 sp, dc in next sc, ch 2, sk next 3 ch**, sc in next ch; rep from * across, ending last rep at **, sc in top of tch, turn.

ROW 7: Ch 3 (count as dc), 2 dc in next ch-2 sp, *dc in next dc, 2 dc in next ch-2 sp; rep from * across to last sc, dc in last sc, turn.

ROW 8: Ch 4 (count as dc, ch 1), sk first 2 dc, *dc in next dc, ch 1, sk next dc; rep from * across to tch, dc in top ch of tch, turn.

Rep Rows 3–8 for patt.

Center Stitch Pattern (csp)

Multiple of 12 sts.

See **Center Stitch Pattern** diagram below for assistance.

FOUNDATION ROW (FOR GAUGE SWATCH ONLY): 36 Fsc, turn.

ROW 1(RS): Ch 1, sc in first sc, *ch 4, sk next 3 sts, sc in next st, ch 5, sk next 2 sts, sc in next st, ch 4, sk next 3 sts**, sc in next st; rep from * across, ending last rep at**, sc in last sc, turn.

ROW 2: Ch 3, *2hdc-cl in next ch-4 sp, ch 3, (2hdc-cl, ch 5, 2hdc-cl) in next ch-5 sp, ch 3, 2hdc-cl in next ch-4 sp **, ch 1; rep from * across ending last rep at**, dc in last sc, turn.

ROW 3: Ch 1, sc in first dc, *3 sc in next ch-3 sp, 5 sc in next ch-5 sp, 3 sc in next ch-3 sp, sc in next ch-1 sp; rep from * across, ending with last sc in top of tch, turn.

ROW 4: Ch 3, sk first sc, * sk next 3 sc, [3hdc-cl in next sc, ch 3] 4 times, 3hdc-cl in next sc, sk next 3 sc, dc in next sc; rep from * across, turn.

ROW 5: Ch 1, sc in first dc, *[sc in next ch-3 sp, ch 4] 3 times, sc in next ch-3 sp**, sc in next dc; rep from * across, ending last rep at **, sc in top ch of tch, turn.

ROW 6: Ch 3, *2hdc-cl in next ch-4 sp, ch 3, (2hdc-cl, ch 5, 2hdc-cl) in next ch-4 sp, ch 3, 2hdc-cl in next ch-4 sp**, ch 1; rep from * across ending last rep at **, dc in last sc, turn.

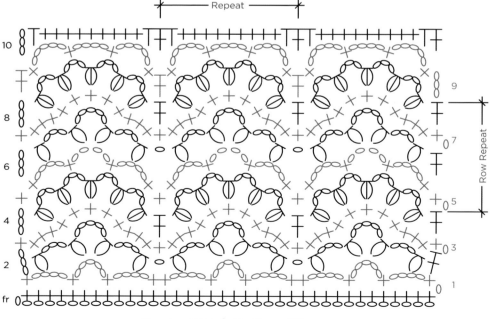

Center Stitch Pattern Diagram

ROWS 7–8: Rep Rows 3–4.

ROW 9: Ch 3, * sc in next ch-3 sp, ch 5, sc in next ch-3 sp, ch 4, sc in next ch-3 sp, ch 5, sc in next ch-3 sp **, dc in next dc; rep form * across, ending last rep at **, dc in top ch of tch, turn.

ROW 10: Ch 3, *(hdc, 2 sc) in next ch-5 sp, sc in next sc, 3 sc in next ch-4 sp, sc in next sc, (2 sc, hdc) in next ch-5 sp **, dc in next dc; rep from * across, ending last rep at **, dc in top ch of tch, turn.

Rep Rows 5–8 for patt.

pattern
Body
Left Side

Fsc 73, turn.

ROW 1 (RS): Work Row 1 of fssp—73 dc.

ROW 2: Work Row 2 of fssp.

Work Rows 3–8 of fssp 7 (8, 9, 10, 11, 12) times.

NEXT ROW: Ch 3 (count as dc), sk first dc, * dc in next ch-1 sp, dc in next dc; rep from * across to tch, dc2tog in top of next 2 ch of tch, turn—72 dc.

NEXT ROW: Ch 1, sc in first and ea st across—72 sc.

Center Panel

Work Rows 1–10 of csp once—73 sts at end of last row.

Right Side

ROW 1: Work Row 1 of fssp—73 dc.

Work Row 2 of fssp.

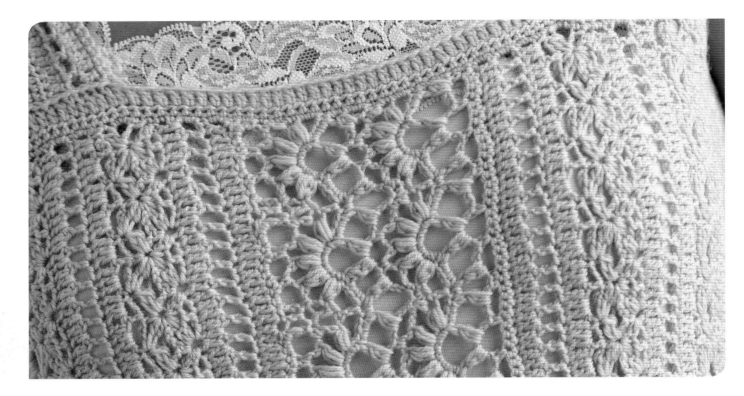

Work Rows 3–8 of fssp 7 (8, 9, 10, 11, 12) times.

Rep Row 3 of fssp once.

NEXT ROW: Ch 1, sc in each dc across.

Fasten off and weave in loose end.

Shoulder Strap (make 2)

Make 2.

Fsc 71 (77, 83, 91, 97, 103) sts.

Work Rows 1–3 of fssp.

ROW 4 (WS): Ch 2 (does not count as a st), hdc in first dc and in each dc across, turn—71 (77, 83, 91, 97, 103) hdc.

ROWS 5–7: Work Rows 1–3 of fssp.

ROW 8: Ch 1, sc in first and ea dc across, turn.

Fasten off.

finishing

Blocking and Seaming

Pin Body and Shoulder straps to schematic measurements (see page 74). Spritz with water and allow to dry.

Pin right sides of Body together at center back. Whipstitch center-back seam together with leftover yarn. Turn RS out.

Upper Edge

With RS facing, join yarn to left-center back upper corner.

ROW 1 (RS): Ch 1, sc evenly across top upper edge to right-center back corner, sl st in first sc to join, turn.

ROW 2: Ch 2 (does not count as a st), hdc in first sc and in ea sc across, sl st in first hdc to join, turn.

ROW 3: Ch 3 (count as dc), sk first hdc, dc in ea hdc across.

Fasten off and weave in end.

Lower Edge

With RS facing, join yarn to right-center back lower corner.

RND 1 (RS): Ch 1, sc evenly across lower edge to left-center back corner, working an even number of sts, sl st in first sc to join, turn.

RND 2: Ch 2 (does not count as a st), hdc in first sc and in ea sc across, sl st in first hdc to join, turn.

RNDS 3–5: Work Rows 1–3 of fssp, joining with a sl st in first st and turning at the end of ea rnd. Rnds 6–7: Rep Row 1 of fssp, joining with a sl st in first st at the end of rnd.

Fasten off and weave in end.

With RS facing and center back seam in back. Pm for ea "side seam" at the top edge. Place shoulder straps at 3 (3¾, 4½, 5¼, 6, 6¼)" (7.5 [9.5, 11.5, 13.5, 15, 16] cm) from ea m on both front and back. Seam shoulder straps to the upper edge.

recycling *yarn*

Have you ever looked at an old sweater in your closet and wondered how you might be able to use the yarn for a new project? Recycling yarn from old projects is relatively simple if you approach the process with a few simple tips in mind.

CHOOSING PIECES TO RECYCLE

Look for pieces that have limited ends so you will have long continuous strands of yarn once the project is raveled. Large men's sweaters and blankets are usually good choices, while projects featuring granny squares are not. If you are going to use a store-bought sweater, look at the seams before taking it home. Sometimes store-bought sweaters feature yarns that are cut at the end of each row, creating lots of short yarn lengths.

DISASSEMBLE

Raveling is easy, but where do you start? If the piece you have chosen is a sweater, take it apart at the seams and separate the front, back, and sleeve panels. Then look for the point where the yarn was fastened off and start raveling from there. Wind the raveling yarn into balls by hand or using a ball winder. Then wind the balls into hanks by winding them around a swift or the back of a chair. Use waste yarn from the seams to tie around the hanks, securing them for the bath.

TAKE A BATH

After all that work, treat your recycled yarn to a spa date. Fill a large bucket with room temperature or cool water and your favorite gentle wool wash. Soak the hanks in the water solution for 30 minutes to help them chill out. Then wrap them in a towel and gently roll out the excess water. Hang hanks to dry with some weight in the bottom of each hank. Weights can be anything from a soup can to a rolled up towel. Allow to dry completely, then wind yarn into balls and crochet your heart out.

sidney cardigan

robyn chachula

Mixing simple construction with a beautifully interesting stitch pattern, this cardigan will be a favorite for years to come. This project is economical so you can crochet several to spoil a special little pumpkin, or share the wealth and give them as gifts to all the little ones in your life. The classic styling and simple shape are sure to make this sweater an instant hit!

MATERIALS

yarn: DK weight (#3 Light).

Shown: Lion Brand, LB Collection Cotton Bamboo (52% cotton, 48% rayon from bamboo; 245 yd [224 m]/ 3.5 oz [100 g]): #174 snapdragon (green), 2 (2, 3, 3) balls.

hook: H/8 (5.0 mm) or hook needed to obtain gauge.

notions: Tapestry needle for weaving in ends; spray bottle with water and straight pins for blocking; one ⅞" (22 mm) button.

GAUGE

20 sts by 8 rows = 4¼" × 4¼" (11 × 11 cm) in Petal Link Stitch Pattern (plsp).

FINISHED SIZE

S (M, L, XL) pullover is sized to fit 6 (12, 18, 24) mos with a relaxed fit. Sample shown is a size XL (24 mos).

finished chest: 20½ (22½, 24¾, 27)" (52 [57, 63, 68.5] cm).

finished length: 12⅞ (12⅞, 16, 16)" (33 [33, 40.5, 40.5] cm).

{notes}

* The top half of the cardigan is crocheted from sleeve to sleeve, and the arms are seamed before continuing the bottom half.

* To extend the life of the garment, it can be worn as a coat with sleeves cuffed one year and as a shorter cardigan with sleeves down the next. Just move the button to adjust for any weight gain.

schematics

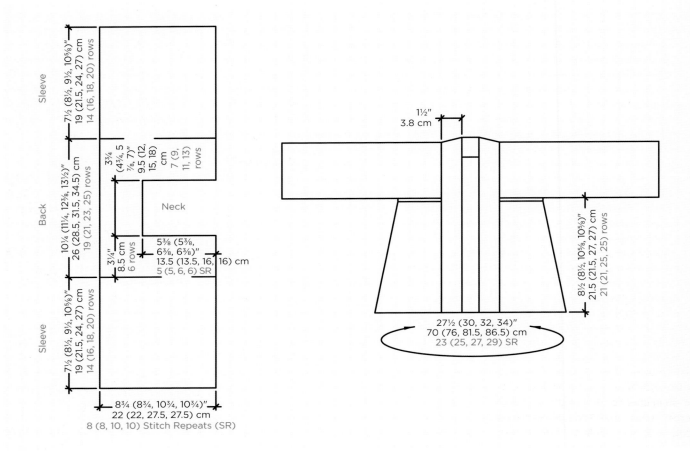

Sleeve
7½ (8½, 9½, 10⅝)" cm
19 (21.5, 24, 27) cm
14 (16, 18, 20) rows

Back
10¼ (11¼, 12⅜, 13½)"
26 (28.5, 31.5, 34.5) cm
19 (21, 23, 25) rows

3¾ (4¾, 5 ⅞, 7)"
9.5 (12, 15, 18) cm
7 (9, 11, 13) rows

Neck

3¼"
8.5 cm
6 rows

5⅜ (5⅜, 6⅜, 6⅜)"
13.5 (13.5, 16, 16) cm
5 (5, 6, 6) SR

Sleeve
7½ (8½, 9½, 10⅝)" cm
19 (21.5, 24, 27) cm
14 (16, 18, 20) rows

8¾ (8¾, 10¾, 10¾)"
22 (22, 27.5, 27.5) cm
8 (8, 10, 10) Stitch Repeats (SR)

1½"
3.8 cm

8½ (8½, 10⅝, 10⅝)" cm
21.5 (21.5, 27, 27) cm
21 (21, 25, 25) rows

27½ (30, 32, 34)"
70 (76, 81.5, 86.5) cm
23 (25, 27, 29) SR

details

Special Stitches

Foundation Single Crochet (fsc): p. 154.

Back Post Double Crochet (BPdc): p. 155.

Shell (sh): (2dc-cl, ch 2, 2dc-cl) in st indicated.

Petal Link Stitch Pattern (plsp)

See **Petal Link Stitch Pattern** diagram above right for assistance.

17 fsc, turn.

ROW 1 (RS): Ch 3 (counts as dc), sk first sc, *sk next sc, sh in next sc, sk next sc, dc in next sc; rep from * across, turn—4 sh.

ROW 2: Ch 3 (counts as dc), *sh in ch-2 sp of next sh, BPdc around next dc; rep from * across to tch, dc in top of tch, turn.

ROW 3: Ch 4 (counts as dc, ch-1 sp), 2dc-cl in first dc, *dc in ch-2 sp of next sh, sh in next dc; rep from * across to last sh, dc in ch-2 sp of last sh, (2dc-cl, ch 1, dc) in top of tch, turn.

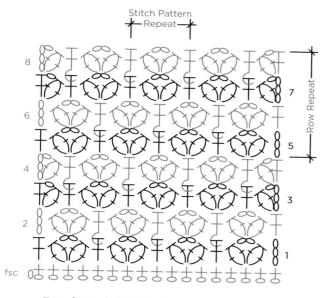

Petal Link Stitch Pattern Diagram

ROW 4: Ch 4 (counts as dc, ch-1 sp), 2dc-cl in first dc, *BPdc around next dc, sh in ch-2 sp of next sh; rep from * across to last sh, BPdc around next dc, (2dc-cl, ch 1, dc) in 3rd ch of tch, turn.

ROW 5: Ch 3 (counts as dc), *sh in next dc, dc in ch-2 sp of next sh; rep from * across to last sh, sh in next dc, dc in 3rd ch of tch, turn.

ROW 6: Ch 3 (counts as dc), *sh in ch-2 sp of next sh, BPdc around next dc; rep from * across to tch, dc in top of tch, turn.

Rep Rows 3–6 for pattern.

pattern
Top Half
First Sleeve

33 (33, 41, 41) fsc, turn.

ROW 1 (RS): Ch 3 (counts as dc), *sk next sc, sh in next sc, sk next sc, dc in next sc; rep from * across, turn—8 (8, 10, 10 sh).

ROW 2: Ch 3 (counts as dc), *sh in ch-2 sp of next sh, BPdc around next dc; rep from * across to tch, dc in top of tch, turn.

Cont in plsp for 18 (20, 22, 24) more rows.

Neck Shaping

ROW 1 (S/L): Cont in plsp for 3 (4) sh, dc in next ch-2 sp of sh, turn.

ROW 1 (M/XL): Cont in plsp for 3 (4) dc, (2 dc-cl, ch 1, dc) in next dc, turn.

Cont in plsp for 5 (7, 9, 11) more rows.

LAST ROW: Cont in plsp across, work 20 (20, 24, 24) fsc, turn.

Second Sleeve

ROW 1: Ch 4 (counts as dc, ch-1 sp), 2dc-cl in first sc, *sk 1 sc, dc in next sc, sk 1 sc, sh in next sc; rep from * across to last sc, cont in plsp across to end, turn—8 (8, 10, 10) dc.

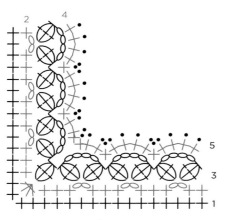

A. Border Diagram

ROW 2: Ch 3 (counts as dc), *sh in next dc, dc in ch-2 sp of next sh; rep from * across to last sh, sh in next dc, dc in 3rd ch of tch, turn.

Cont in plsp for 18 (20, 22, 24) more rows.

LAST ROW: Ch 1, sc in first st, work 2 sc in each ch-2 sp and 2 sc in each dc across, sc in tch. Fasten off.

Pin top half to schematic size (see Schematics on page 82) and spray with water bottle to block. Pin RS of arm seams together. Whipstitch sleeve seams together, see schematic for length of sleeves.

Bottom Edging

ROW 1: With RS facing, join yarn on bottom edge at lower left-hand corner of left front, ch 1, work 93 (101, 109, 117) sc evenly spaced across bottom edge of body to bottom right-hand corner of right front, turn.

ROW 2: Ch 1, sc in each sc across, turn.

Bottom Half

ROW 1 (RS): Ch 3 (counts as dc), sk first sc, *sk next sc, sh in next sc, sk next sc, dc in next sc; rep from * across, turn—23 (25, 27, 29) sh.

ROW 2: Ch 3 (counts as dc), *sh in ch-2 sp of next sh, BPdc around next dc; rep from * across to tch, dc in top of tch, turn.

Cont in plsp for 14 (14, 18, 18) more rows.

Edging

ROW 1: Ch 1, sc in first st, work 2 sc in each ch-2 sp and 2 sc in each dc across, sc in last st, turn.

ROW 2: Ch 1, sc in each st around, turn.

ROW 3: Sl st in each sc around. Fasten off. Weave in ends.

Finishing
Cuff Edging

With RS facing, join yarn to edge of cuff, ch 1, sc evenly around cuff edge, join with sl st in first sc. Fasten off. Rep Cuff Edging around other cuff edge. Pin cardigan to schematic size (see Schematics on page 82), spray with water to block, and allow to dry. With RS facing, join yarn to RS of top half, sl st in each sc around top half, fasten off, weave in ends.

Neck Border

With RS facing, join yarn in bottom right-hand corner of right front edge. See **Stitch Diagram A** at far left for assistance.

ROW 1: Ch 1, sc evenly up edge of right front edge, working a multiple of 4 sts, turn 90 degrees, sc evenly across back neck edge working a multiple of 4 plus 3 sts, turn 90 degrees, sc down front edge in a multiple of 4 sts (equal to right front edge), turn.

ROW 2: Ch 1, sc in first 2 sc, *ch 2, sk next sc, sc in next 3 sc*; rep from * across to last 2 sc before corner of neck, sc4tog over 4 sc at corner of neck, sc in next 3 sc; rep from * to * across neck to last 2 sc before opposite corner, sc4tog over 4 sc at corner of neck, sc in next 3 sc; rep from * across to last 2 sc, sc in last 2 sc, turn.

ROW 3: Ch 3 (counts as dc), ** *(3dc-cl, ch 4, 3dc-cl) in ea ch-2 sp across to next corner*, 3dc-cl in next sc4tog at corner; rep from ** once; rep from * to * to end, dc in last sc, turn.

ROW 4: Ch 1, sc in dc, ** *4 sc in ch-4 sp, sc bet next two 3dc-cl*; rep from * to ch-sp before neck corner, 3 sc in next 2 ch-4 sp (skipping 3dc-cl); rep from ** once; rep from * to * to end, sc in top of tch, turn.

ROW 5: Sl st in each sc across. Fasten off. Weave in ends.

Sew button to center of border at seam of top half using the photo at right as a guide. Use one of spaces in border as buttonhole.

4 – 5
balls

dots and dashes baby blanket

ellen gormley

Modular and modern, this baby blanket will be the highlight of a baby's collection. With a quick color change, this project can be customized for a girl, a boy, or even an adult. Because of the building-block style of the motifs, the blanket can easily be made in larger or smaller sizes.

MATERIALS

yarn: Worsted weight (#4 Medium).

Shown: Caron, Simply Soft (100% acrylic; 315 yd [288 m]/6 oz [170 g]): #9754 persimmon (MC), 2 balls; #9719 soft pink (CC1), 2 balls; #9723 raspberry (CC2), 1 ball.

hook: I/9 (6 mm) or hook needed to obtain gauge.

notions: Tapestry needle for weaving in ends; spray bottle with water and straight pins for blocking.

GAUGE

Square motif = 4" × 4" (10 × 10 cm) in stitch pattern.

Rectangle motif = 4" × 5" (10 cm × 13 cm) in stitch pattern.

FINISHED SIZE

37" × 37" (94 × 94 cm).

{note}

* All rounds are worked on the RS and are joined and not turned.

pattern

Square Motif

Refer to **Stitch Diagram A** at right for assistance.

Make 16 ea of Motifs A and B as follows.

Motif A

RND 1: CC1.

RND 2: CC1.

RND 3: MC.

RND 4: CC2.

Motif B

RND 1: MC.

RND 2: MC.

RND 3: CC2.

RND 4: CC1.

With first color, ch 5; join with sl st to form a ring.

RND 1: Ch 4 (counts as first tr), 17 more tr in ring; join with sl st in top beg ch-4—18 tr.

RND 2: Ch 3 (counts as first dc), dc in same st, 2 dc in ea st around; join with sl st in top beg ch-3—36 dc. Fasten off.

RND 3: With RS facing, join next color with sl st in any st, ch 3 (counts as dc), 2 dc in same st; *dc in next st, hdc in next st, sc in next 4 sts, hdc in next st, dc in next st**, 3 dc in next st; rep from * twice; rep from * to ** once; join with sl st in top beg ch-3—20 dc, 8 hdc, 16 sc. Fasten off.

RND 4: With RS facing, join next color with sc in middle sc of any sc-3 corner, 2 sc in same st; *sc in ea of next 10 sts, 3 sc in next st; rep from * twice, sc in ea of last 10 sts; join with sl st in first sc—52 sc. Fasten off.

Rectangle Motif

Refer to **Stitch Diagram B** at far right for assistance.

Make 16 ea of Motifs C and D as follows.

Motif C

RND 1: CC2.

RND 2: CC1.

RND 3: MC.

RND 4: CC1.

RND 5: MC.

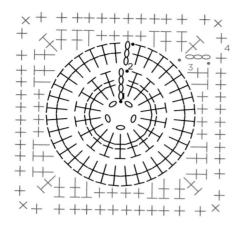

A. Square Motif Diagram

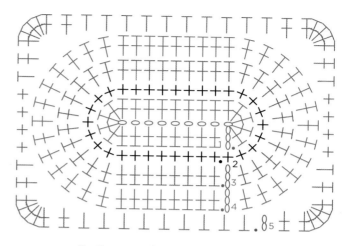

B. Rectangle Motif Diagram

Motif D

RND 1: MC.

RND 2: CC2.

RND 3: CC1.

RND 4: MC.

RND 5: CC1.

With first color, ch 12.

RND 1: 5 dc in 4th ch from hook, dc in ea of next 7 sts, 6 dc in last ch, working along foundation ch, dc in ea of next 7 sts; join with sl st in 11th ch, which is the top of the first dc. Fasten off—26 dc.

RND 2: With RS facing, join next color with sc in first dc of 6-dc end, [2 sc in next st, sc in next st] twice, 2 sc in next st, sc in ea of next 8 sts, [2 sc in next st, sc in next st] twice, 2 sc in next st, sc in ea of last 7 sts; join with sl st in first sc. Fasten off—32 sc.

RND 3: With RS facing, join next color with sl st in st where previously fastened off, ch 3 (counts as dc); *[2 dc in next st, dc in next 2 sts] 3 times*, dc in next 7 sts; rep from * to * once, dc in last 6 sts; join with sl st in top of beg ch-3—38 dc. Fasten off.

RND 4: With RS facing, join next color with sl st in st where previously fastened off, ch 3 (counts as dc), dc in next 2 sts; *[2 dc in next st, dc in ea of next 3 sts] 3 times*, dc in ea of next 7 sts; rep from * to * once, dc in last 4 sts; join with sl st in top beg ch-3. Fasten off—44 dc.

RND 5: With RS facing, join next color with sl st where previously fastened off, ch 2 (counts as hdc), *dc in next st, 5 dc in next st, dc in next st, hdc in next st, sc in ea of next 4 sts, hdc in next st, dc in next st, 5 dc in next st, dc in next st*, hdc in ea of next 10 sts; rep from * to * once, hdc in ea of last 9 sts; join with sl st in top beg ch-2. Fasten off—60 sts.

Circle inserts

Make 4.

With CC1, ch 3; join with sl st in first ch to form ring.

RND 1: Ch 3, (counts as dc), 11 more dc in ring; join with sl st in beg ch-3—12 dc. Fasten off, leaving an 18″ (45.5 cm) tail for sewing.

Assembly

Refer to the Construction Diagram on page 92 for assistance. Pin motifs to finished measurements (see gauge on page 89). Spritz with water and allow to dry.

32 Pairs of Motifs

With MC and RS facing, working through outer loops only and matching stitches, sc Motif A with short side of Motif C. Rep to make 15 more pairs. Rep the same process with Motif B and the short side of Motif D to make 16 pairs.

16 Units of 4 motifs

With CC1 and RS facing, working through outer lps only and matching sts, sc the A/C pair to the B/D pair. Rep for the rem 15 units.

4 Quadrants

The 4 quadrants of the blanket are identical. Each quadrant uses 4 of the Units. Working clockwise from top left, the first unit is vertical, the next unit to the right is horizontal, the next unit below right is vertical, and the last unit at bottom left is horizontal. With CC1 and RS facing, working through outer loops only and matching sts, working from the outer edge toward the middle empty space where the CC1 circle insert will go, sc 2 Units together. Rep 3 more times until the quadrant is completed. Rep entire process 3 more times until all 4 quadrants are completed. In same manner, sc the quadrants together.

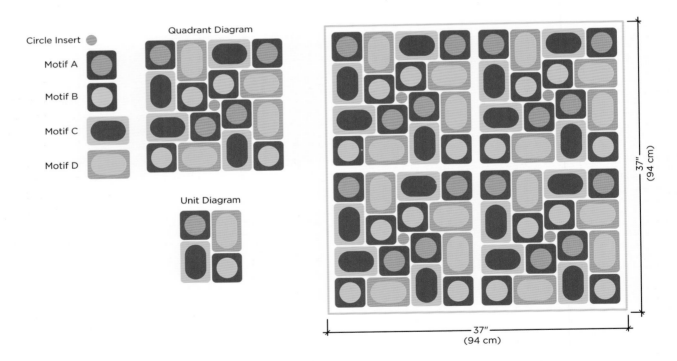

Construction Diagram

Attach Circle Inserts

With CC1 and tapestry needle and WS facing, hold the insert in the empty space left by the Units, using the long tail, whipstitch the insert into the empty space by whipstitching it to its adjacent neighbors. There are 12 insert stitches and 4 neighboring motifs, ea motif will attach to the insert in 3 of the insert's stitches.

Edging and Finishing

RND 1: With RS facing, join CC1 with sc in middle sc st of any corner, 2 more sc in same st; *sc in ea st to next corner, 3 sc in middle st of next corner; rep from * twice, sc in ea st to end; join with sl st in first sc—516 sc. Fasten off.

RND 2: With RS facing, join MC with sl st in middle sc of any corner, ch 4 (counts as first tr), 8 more tr in same st; *sk next 3 sts, sc in ea st across to last 4 sts of side, sk next 3 sts, 9 tr in middle sc of 3-sc corner; rep from * twice, sc in ea st across to last 3 sts, sk next 3 sts; join with sl st in top beg ch-4—488 sc, 36 tr. Fasten off.

Weave in ends.

Ellen Gormley stitched more than eighty afghans before beginning her design career in 2004. Now, she has sold more than 100 designs and been published numerous times in crochet magazines such as *Interweave Crochet*, *Crochet Today*, *Crochet!*, *Crochet World*, and *Inside Crochet*. Her designs have been shown on the PBS show *Knit and Crochet Now!* Her first book, *Go Crochet! Afghan Design Workbook*, was released in May 2011 from F+W/ Krause publishers.

If you had only one ball of yarn... I'd make a short scarf or cowl. I'd want a piece that I could wear near my face, worked in a bright, flattering color to offer a splash of vibrancy during cold winters.

tallula baby top

marlaina bird

The timeless beauty of crocheted motifs, coupled with the simple texture of the griddle stitch, makes this a perfect piece for every little girl. It is pretty without being too fussy or frilly, and it looks great worn with simple trousers or a skirt. Work one up in the recipient's favorite color for a gift that will be well loved.

{notes}

* Motifs are joined as you go after the first one is made.

* Top portion is worked in the round to armholes, then separated for front and back.

* Buttons should be added with caution as they could be a choking hazard for young children if they were to come off the garment. As an alternative, you may omit buttonholes and buttons and seam both shoulders.

* In Griddle Stitch pattern "as est" work as follows:
  • In first stitch, work an sc or dc, as needed, to maintain an alternating pattern of sc and dc.
  • Work an sc in each dc and a dc in each sc across, and continue the alternating pattern of sc and dc all the way across to the last stitch.

MATERIALS
yarn: Sportweight (#2 Fine).

Shown: Spud and Chloe, Fine (80% wool 20% silk; 248 yds [227 m]/2.29 oz [65 g]): #7807 tutu, 2 (2, 3, 4) balls.

hook: C/2 (2.75 mm) and D/3 (3.25 mm) or hook needed to obtain gauge.

notions: Stitch marker; tapestry needle for weaving in ends; four ⅜" (9 mm) buttons; matching thread and handsewing needle, spray bottle with water and straight pins for blocking.

GAUGE
24 sts by 22½ rows = 4" × 4" (10 × 10 cm) in Griddle stitch pattern with smaller hook.

20 sts by 24 rows = 4" × 4" (10 × 10 cm) in Griddle stitch pattern with larger hook.

Mudan Motif = 4" wide by 4½" tall (10 × 11.5 cm).

Peony Motif = 4" wide by 3" tall (10 × 7.5 cm).

FINISHED SIZE
S (M, L, XL) pullover is sized to fit sizes 2 (4, 6, 8) years with a tight fit. Sample shown is a size M (4 years).

finished Chest: 19¼ (20, 25½, 26½)" (49 [51, 65, 67.5] cm).

finished length: 16 (16¾, 18, 18¾)" (40.5 [42.5, 45.5, 47.5] cm).

schematic

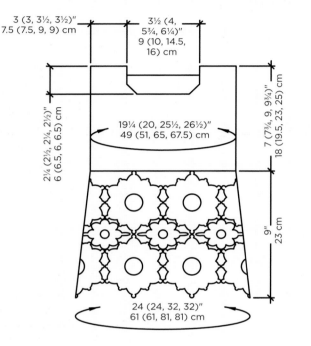

3 (3, 3½, 3½)"
7.5 (7.5, 9, 9) cm

3½ (4, 5¾, 6¼)"
9 (10, 14.5, 16) cm

2¼ (2½, 2¼, 2½)"
6 (6.5, 6, 6.5) cm

19¼ (20, 25½, 26½)"
49 (51, 65, 67.5) cm

7 (7¾, 9, 9¾)"
18 (19.5, 23, 25) cm

9"
23 cm

24 (24, 32, 32)"
61 (61, 81, 81) cm

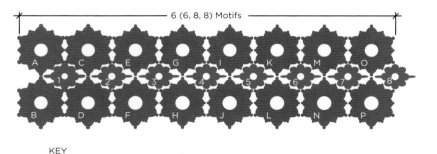

6 (6, 8, 8) Motifs

A C E G I K M O
1 2 3 4 5 6 7 8
B D F H J L N P

Construction Diagram

KEY

Mudan Motif

Peony Motif

details

Special Stitch

Shell (sh): (Sc, hdc, 2 dc, ch 2, 2 dc, hdc, sc) in st indicated.

Griddle Stitch Pattern in Rows (gsp)

Refer to the **Griddle Stitch Pattern** diagram at right for assistance.

(Multiple of 2 sts)

SETUP ROW: Sc in 2nd ch from hook, *dc in next ch, sc in next ch; rep from * to last ch, dc in last ch, turn.

ROW 1: Ch 1 (does not count as st), *sc in next dc, dc in next sc; rep from * across to last st, dc in last st.

Repeat this row for Griddle Stitch Pattern (gsp).

pattern

Lower Body

The lower body is made up of motifs. Make first motif to completion, then work 4 (4, 6, 6) more Mudan Motifs across, joining to previous motif with sl st in 3 corresponding ch-sps while completing Rnd 5. Then join last motif to previous motif and first motif in 3 corresponding ch-sps on each side, while completing Rnd 5. Make and join 6 (6, 8, 8) more Mudan Motifs to each other and to first ring of motifs in same manner. Follow the stitch diagrams for joining.

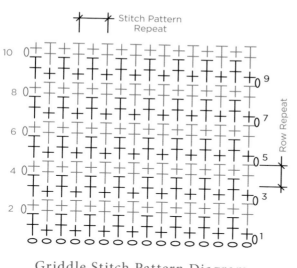

Griddle Stitch Pattern Diagram

A. Mudan Motif

First Mudan Motif (make 1)

Refer to **Stitch Diagram A** at far right for assistance.

With smaller hook, ch 6, join with a sl st in first ch.

RND 1 (RS): Ch 1, 12 sc in ring, join with a sl st in first sc—12 sc.

RND 2: Ch 7 (counts as dc, ch 4), sk 1 sc, [dc in next sc, ch 4, sk 1 sc] 4 times, sk 1 sc, dc in next sc, ch 1, dc in 3rd ch of beg ch instead of last ch-4 sp.

RND 3: Ch 5 (counts as, ch 2), (2 dc, hdc, sc) in first sp, sh in each of next 5 ch-4 sps, (sc, hdc, dc) in first sp, join with sl st in 3rd ch of beg ch.

RND 4: Sl st in next ch-2 sp, ch 4 (counts as tr), 4 tr in same ch-2 sp, 9 tr in next 5 ch-2 sps, 4 tr in first 2-ch sp, join with a sl st to 3rd ch of beg ch, do not turn.

RND 5: Ch 8 (counts as dc, ch 5), 2 dc in first tr, *ch 2, sk 2 tr, sc in next tr, ch 2, sk 1 tr, (dc, ch 3, dc) in sp bet 9-tr groups of prev row, ch 2, sk 1 tr, sc in next tr, ch 2**, sk 2 tr, (2 dc, ch 5, 2 dc) in next tr; rep from * 4 times; rep from * to ** once, dc in first tr of prev rnd, join with sl st in 3rd ch of beg ch-8. Fasten off.

Joining of Second and Successive Mudan Motifs

Make and join 11 more Modal Motifs, joining each to previous motif(s) while completing Rnd 5. Work same as First Mudan Motif through Rnd 4. See Stitch Diagram B on p. 99 for Joining and refer to the Construction Diagram on p. 96 for assistance.

RND 5 (JOINING RND): Work same as Rnd 5 of First Mudan Motif, joining

corresponding ch-5 sps by working (ch 2, sl st in corresponding ch-5 sp on previous motif, ch 2) instead of ch-5 sps and joining corresponding ch-3 sps by working (ch 1, sl st in corresponding ch-3 sp on previous motif, ch 1) instead of ch-3 sps. Join 4 (4, 6, 6) motifs in a strip, joining to (ch-5 sp, ch3 sp, ch-5 sp) on right side of motif, then join next motif in (ch-5 sp, ch-3 sp, ch-5 sp) across side of previous motif and first motif of strip to form a ring. Join one motif to first motif of first ring of motifs, by joining with sl st in bottom ch-5 sp. Join 4 more motifs in second strip to previous motif and to first ring of motifs in same manner.

Peony Motif:

Refer to **Stitch Diagram B** at right for assistance.

Make and join 6 (6, 8, 8) motifs between joined Mudan Motifs.

Ch 8, join with a sl st to the first ch.

RND 1 (RS): Rnd 1 (RS): Ch 1, 16 sc in ring, join with a sl st to first sc—16 sc.

RND 2: Ch 7 (counts as dc and ch-4), sk 1 sc, [dc in next sc, ch 4, sk 1 sc] 7 times, join with a sl st to the 3rd ch of beg ch.

RND 3: Ch 1, *(sc, hdc, 2 dc, ch 1, sl st in junction between 2 Mudan Motifs in top ring of motifs, ch 1, 2 dc, hdc, sc) in next ch-4 sp on current motif, sk next 2 ch-2 sps, (sc, hdc, 2 dc, ch 1, sl st in next ch-3 sp on adjacent Mudan Motif, ch 1, 2 dc, hdc, sc) in next ch-4 sp on current motif, sk next 2 ch-2 sps, (sc, hdc, 2 dc, ch 3, sl st in junction between to 2 Mudan Motifs, ch 3, 2 dc, hdc, sc) in next ch-4 sp on current motif, (sc, hdc, 2 dc, ch 1, sl st in next ch-3 sp on adjacent Mudan Motif on bottom ring of motifs, ch 1, 2 dc, hdc, sc) in next ch-4 sp on current motif, sk next 2 ch-2 sps; rep from * once, join with sl st in first sc. Fasten off.

B. Joining and Peony Motif

Upper Body

For this portion of the sweater only, use larger hook for sizes S and L only; use smaller hook for sizes M and XL only.

FOUNDATION RND (RS): Join yarn with a sl st in ch-5 sp at the top of any motif on top edge of Lower Body, ch 1, *sc in 5-ch sp, ch 3 (4, 3, 4), sk next 2 ch-2 sps, 5dc-cl in next 3-ch sp, ch 3 (4, 3, 4), sk next 2 ch-2 sps, 5tr-cl in junction between next 2 motifs ch 3 (4, 3, 4), sk next 2 ch-2 sps, 5dc-cl in next ch-3 sp, ch 3 (4, 3, 4) sk next 2 ch-2 sps; rep from * around, join with sl st in first sc, turn—24 (24, 32, 32) ch-sps.

RND 1 (WS): Ch 1, sc in first st, dc in next st, *sc in next st, dc in next st; rep from * around treating each ch, sc, 5dc-cl, and 5tr-cl as a st, join with sl st in first sc, turn—96 (120, 128, 160) sts.

RND 2 (RS): Ch 1, *sc in next dc, dc in next sc; rep from * around, join with sl st in first sc, turn.

Rep Rnd 2 until upper body measures 2½ (3, 3½, 4)″ (6.5 [7.5, 9, 10] cm) from beginning.

Front
Armhole Opening

Separate for front and back.

ROW 1: Work in gsp over first 48 (60, 64, 80) sts, turn.

Work even in gsp until armhole measures 2 (2½, 3, 3½)″ (5 [6.5, 7.5, 9] cm) ending with a WS row.

Neck Opening and Shoulder

Work each shoulder at the same time here to end with separate balls of yarn.

ROW 1 (RS): Work in gsp across for first 19 (21, 22, 24) sts, sk next 10 (18, 20, 32) sts, join new ball of yarn in next st with a sl st, ch 1, work in gsp across to end of row, turn—19 (21, 22, 24) sts on each side.

Work 8 more rows in gsp on each shoulder, dec 1 st by working sc2tog at neck edge on next row and every other row 3 more times—15 (17, 18, 20) sts rem at shoulder.

Pm on this row at either end, work even in gsp for 5 more rows, fasten off.

Back
Armhole Opening

ROW 1: With appropriate side facing, join yarn in first st to the left of last st made in Front, ch 1, work in gsp across 48 (60, 64, 80) sts, turn.

Work even in gsp until Back armhole measures same as Front armhole to stitch marker.

Neck Opening and Shoulder

Work each shoulder at the same time here to end with separate balls of yarn.

ROW 1 (WS): Work in gsp across first 15 (17, 18, 20) sts, sk next 24 (30, 32, 40) sts, join new ball of yarn in next st with

a sl st, ch 1, work in gsp across to end of row, turn—15 (17, 18, 20) sts each side.

Work even in gsp for 5 more rows, turn.

Right Shoulder Only (optional)

BUTTONHOLE ROW (RS): Ch 1, sc in first 1 (2, 3, 4) sts, *ch 3, sk 1 st, sc in each of next 3 sts; rep from * twice, ch 3, sk 1 st, sc in each rem st across—4 ch-3 buttonholes. Fasten off.

Left Shoulder

JOINING ROW (RS): Pin right sides of Front and Back together at shoulder, matching sts, ch 1, working through double thickness, sl st in each st across. Fasten off.

Rep Joining Row on right shoulder if omitting buttonholes.

Finishing

Weave in all loose ends. Pin piece to finished measurements (refer to the Schematics on page 96). Spritz with water and allow to dry. Using sewing needle and thread, sew buttons to right front shoulder opposite buttonholes on back shoulder.

amelia cardigan

julia vaconsin

This sweet cardigan is a great gift for your favorite little girl. It features a large cable pattern and a wide edging on rounded front edges for visual interest. This sweater will keep your little one warm and cozy, while the cardigan style makes it easy to put on and take off quickly.

MATERIALS

yarn: Sportweight (#2 fine).

Shown: Filatura di Crosa, Zarina (100% Merino superwash wool; 180 yd [165 m]/1.75 oz [50 g]): #433 royal purple, 3 (3, 4, 4) balls.

hook: G/6 (4 mm) or hook needed to obtain gauge.

notions: Pins for blocking; tapestry needle for seaming and weaving in ends; three ⅝" (15 mm) snap fasteners.

GAUGE

19 sc by 19 rows = 4" × 4" (10 × 10 cm) in single crochet.

FINISHED SIZE

S (M, L, XL) to fit 6 (12, 18, 24) mos. Cardigan shown is a size XL (24 mos).

finished chest: 20 (21, 22, 23½)" (51 [53.5, 56, 59.5] cm).

finished length: 12 (12¾, 13¾, 14½)" (30.5 [32, 35, 37] cm).

NOTE

Pattern works over 2 charts in the same row. Sticky notes make great place markers for keeping track of where you are in the pattern.

schematics

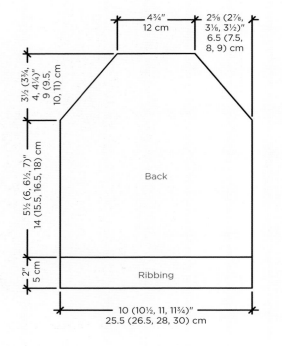

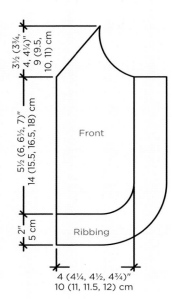

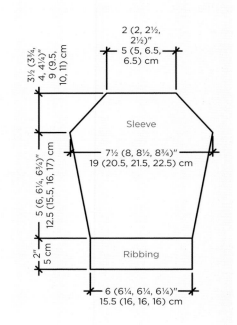

details

Special Stitches

Single Crochet 2 Together (sc2tog):
p. 154.

Front Post Double Crochet (FPdc):
p. 155.

Front Post Treble Crochet (FPtr): Yo twice, insert hook from front to back to front again around the post of designated st, yo, draw yarn through, [yo, draw yarn through 2 lps on hook] 3 times, sk st behind FPtr just made.

4-FPdc crochet cable (dc-cable): Sk next 2 FP sts 2 rows below, FPdc in next 2 FP sts 2 rows below, working over the 2 FPdc just made, FPdc in last 2 skipped FP sts, sk 4 sts behind cable just made.

4-FPtr Crochet Cable in Front (tr-cable-front): Sk next 2 FP sts 2 rows below, FPtr in next 2 FP sts 2 rows below, working over the 2 FPtr just made, FPtr in last 2 skipped FP sts, sk 4 sts behind cable just made.

4-FPtr Crochet Cable in Back (tr-cable-back): Sk next 2 FP sts 2 rows below, FPtr in next 2 FP sts 2 rows below, working underneath the 2 FPtr just made, FPtr in last 2 skipped FP sts, sk 4 sts behind cable just made.

Cable Pattern A

Refer to **Stitch Diagram A** on page 106 for assistance.

Ch 15.

Foundation Row (WS): Sc in 2nd ch and in ea ch across, turn—14 sc.

ROW 1 (RS): Sc in next 3 sts, FPdc around next 2 sts, sc in next 4 sts, FPdc around next 2 sts, sc in next 3 sts.

ROW 2 AND ALL EVEN ROWS: Sc in ea st across.

ROW 3: Sc in next 4 sts, FPdc around ea of next 2 FP sts, sc in next 2 sts, FPdc around ea of next 2 FP sts, sc in next 4 sts.

ROW 5: Sc in next 5 sts, FPdc around ea of next 4 FP sts, sc in next 5 sts.

ROW 7: Work as Row 5.

ROW 9: Work as Row 3.

ROW 11: Work as Row 1.

ROW 13: Sc in next 2 sts, FPdc around ea of next 2 FP sts, sc in next 6 sts, FPdc around ea of next 2 FP sts, sc in next 2 sts.

ROW 14: Sc in ea st across, turn.

Rep Rows 1–14 for pattern.

Cable Pattern B

Refer to **Stitch Diagram B** on page 106 for assistance.

Ch 17.

FOUNDATION ROW (WS): Sc in 2nd ch and in ea ch across, turn—16 sc.

ROW 1 (RS): Sc in next 2 sts, FPdc around next 2 sts, sc in next 2 sts, FPdc around next 4 sts, sc in next 2 sts, FPdc around next 2 sts, sc in next 2 sts.

ROW 2 AND ALL EVEN ROWS: Sc in ea st across.

ROW 3: Sc in next 2 sts, FPdc around next 2 sts, sc in next 2 sts, dc-cable over next 4 sts 2 rows below, sc in next 2 sts, FPdc around next 2 sts, sc in next 2 sts.

ROW 5: Work as Row 1.

ROW 7: Work as Row 3.

ROW 9: Sc in first 3 sts, FPdc around ea of last 2 FP sts, FPdc around first 2 sts of middle cable, sc in next 2 sts, FPdc around 3rd and 4th sts of middle cable, FPdc around ea of next 2 FP sts, sc in next 3 sts.

ROW 11: Sc in first 3 sts, tr-cable-back over next 4 sts 2 rows below, sc in next 2 sts, tr-cable-front, sc in last 3 sts.

ROW 13: Sc in next 2 sts, FPdc around ea of next 2 FP sts, sc in next 2 sts, FPdc around ea of next 4 FP sts, sc in next 2 sts, FPdc around ea of next 2 FP sts, sc in last 2 sts.

ROW 14: Sc in ea st across.

Rep Rows 1–14 for pattern.

pattern
Back

Ch 49 (51, 53, 57).

ROW 1 (RS): Sc in 2nd ch from hook and in each ch across, turn—48 (50, 52, 56) sc.

ROW 2: Ch 1, sc in ea st across, turn.

ROW 3: Ch 1, sc in ea of first 2 (3, 4, 6) sc, work Row 1 of **Cable Chart A**, then Row 1 of **Cable Chart B**, then Row 1 of **Cable Chart A** again, sc in ea of last 2 (3, 4, 6) sc, turn.

ROW 4: Ch 1, sc in ea st across, turn.

ROW 5: Ch 1, sc in ea of first 2 (3, 4, 6) sc, work Row 3 of **Cable Chart A**, then Row 3 of **Cable Chart B**, then Row 3 of **Cable Chart A** again, sc in ea of last 2 (3, 4, 6) sc, turn.

Starting with Row 4 of charts, work even in est patt for 22 (24, 26, 28) more rows, ending with Row 10 (12, 14, 2) of charts—26 (28, 30, 32) rows total.

Start Raglan Decreases

ROW 1: Ch 1, sk first st, sc in next 1 (2, 3, 5) sts, work Row 11 (13, 1, 3) of **Cable Chart A**, work Row 11 (13, 1, 3) of **Cable Chart B**, work Row 11 (13, 1, 3) of **Cable Chart A** again, sc in next 0 (1, 2, 4) sts,

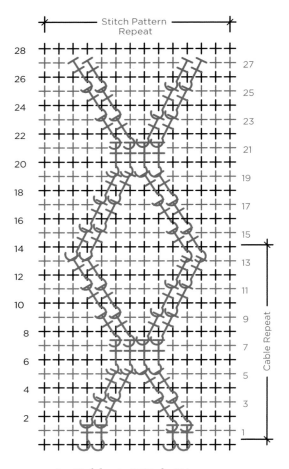

A. Cable A Stitch Diagram

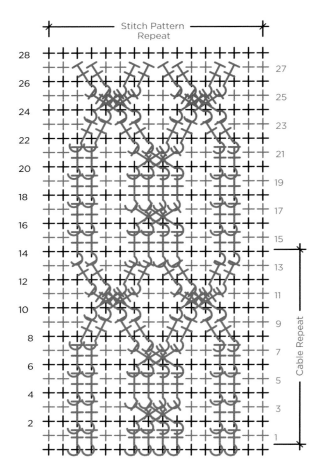

B. Cable B Stitch Diagram

sc2tog over last 2 sts, turn—46 (48, 50, 54) sts.

ROW 2: Ch 1, sk first st, sc in ea st across to last 2 sts, sc2tog over last 2 sts, turn—44 (46, 48, 52) sts.

SIZE S ONLY:

ROW 3: Ch 1, sk first st, sc in next st, FPdc around ea of next 2 FP sts, sc in next 6 sts, FPdc around ea of next 2

FP sts, sc in next 2 sts, work Row 13 of **Cable Chart B,** sc in next 2 sts, FPdc around ea of next 2 FP sts, sc in next 6 sts, FPdc around ea of next 2 FP sts, sc2tog over last 2 sts, turn—42 sts.

ROW 4: Ch 1, sc in ea st across, turn.

ROW 5: Ch 1, sk first st, sc in next st, FPdc around ea of next 2 FP sts, sc in next 4 sts, FPdc around ea of next 2

FP sts, sc in next 3 sts, work Row 1 of **Cable Chart B,** sc in next 3 sts, FPdc around ea of next 2 FP sts, sc in next 4 sts, FPdc around ea of next 2 FP sts, sc2tog over last 2 sts, turn—40 sts.

ROW 6: Work as Row 2—38 sts.

ROW 7: Ch 1, sk first st, FPdc around ea of next 2 FP sts, sc in next 2 sts, FPdc around ea of next 2 FP sts, sc in next

4 sts, work Row 3 of **Cable Chart B,** sc in next 4 sts, FPdc around ea of next 2 FP sts, sc in next 2 sts, FPdc around ea of next 2 FP sts, turn—36 sts.

ROW 8: Work as Row 4.

ROW 9: Ch 1, sk first st, FPdc around ea of next 4 FP sts, sc in next 5 sts, work Row 5 of **Cable Chart B,** sc in next 5 sts, FPdc around ea of next 4 FP sts, turn—34 sts.

ROW 10: Work as Row 2—32 sts.

ROW 11: Ch 1, sk first st, FPdc around ea of next 2 FP sts, sc in next 5 sts, work Row 7 of **Cable Chart B,** sc in next 5 sts, FPdc around each of next 2 FPdc, turn—30 sts.

ROW 12: Work as Row 4.

ROW 13: Ch 1, sk first st, sc in next 6 sts, work Row 9 of **Cable Chart B,** sc in next 5 sts, sc2tog over last 2 sts, turn—28 sts.

ROW 14: Work as Row 2—26 sts.

ROW 15: Ch 1, sk first st, sc in next 4 sts, work Row 11 of **Cable Chart B,** sc in next 3 sts, sc2tog over last 2 sts, turn—24 sts.

ROW 16: Work as Row 4.

ROW 17: Ch 1, sk first st, sc in next 3 sts, work Row 13 of **Cable Chart B,** sc in next 2 sts, sc2tog.

Fasten off.

SIZE M ONLY:

ROW 3: Ch 1, sk first st, sc in next 3 sts, FPdc around ea of next 2 FP sts, sc in next 4 sts, FPdc around ea of next 2 FP sts, sc in next 3 sts, work Row 1 of **Cable Chart B,** sc in next 3 sts, FPdc

around ea of next 2 FP sts, sc in next 4 sts, FPdc around ea of next 2 FP sts, sc in next 2 sts, sc2tog over last 2 sts, turn—44 sts.

ROW 4: Ch 1, sc in ea st across, turn.

ROW 5: Ch 1, sk first st, sc in next 3 sts, FPdc around ea of next 2 FP sts, sc in next 2 sts, FPdc around ea of next 2 FP sts, sc in next 4 sts, work Row 3 of **Cable Chart B,** sc in next 4 sts, FPdc around ea of next 2 FP sts, sc in next 2 sts, FPdc around ea of next 2 FP sts, sc in next 2 sts, sc2tog over last 2 sts, turn—42 sts.

ROW 6: Work as Row 2—40 sts.

ROW 7: Ch 1, sk first st, sc in next 2 sts, FPdc around ea of next 4 FP sts, sc in next 5 sts, work Row 5 of **Cable Chart B,** sc in next 5 sts, FPdc around ea of next 4 FP sts, sc in next st, sc2tog over last 2 sts, turn—38 sts.

ROW 8: Work as Row 4.

ROW 9: Ch 1, sk first st, sc in next st, FPdc around ea of next 4 FP sts, sc in next 5 sts, work Row 7 of **Cable Chart B,** sc in next 5 sts, FPdc around ea of next 4 FP sts, sc2tog over last 2 sts, turn—36 sts.

ROW 10: Work as Row 2—34 sts.

ROW 11: Ch 1, sk first st, sc in next 2 sts, FPdc around ea of next 2 FP sts, sc in next 4 sts, work Row 9 of **Cable Chart B,** sc in next 4 sts, FPdc around ea of next 2 FP sts, sc in next st, sc2tog over last 2 sts, turn—32 sts.

ROW 12: Work as Row 4.

ROW 13: Ch 1, sk first st, sc in next 2 sts, FPdc around ea of next 2 FP sts, sc in

next 3 sts, work Row 11 of **Cable Chart B,** sc in next 3 sts, FPdc around ea of next 2 FP sts, sc in next st, sc2tog over last 2 sts, turn—30 sts.

ROW 14: Work as Row 2—28 sts.

ROW 15: Ch 1, sk first st, sc in next st, FPdc around ea of next 2 FP sts, sc in next 2 sts, work Row 13 of **Cable Chart B,** sc in next 2 sts, FPdc around next 2 sts, sc2tog over last 2 sts, turn—26 sts.

ROW 16: Work as Row 4.

ROW 17: Ch 1, sk first st, sc in next 4 sts, work Row 1 of **Cable Chart B,** sc in next 3 sts, sc2tog over last 2 sts, turn—24 sts.

ROW 18: Work as Row 2—22 sts.

Fasten off.

SIZE L ONLY:

ROW 3: Ch 1, sk first st, sc in next st, work Row 3 of **Cable Charts A, B** and **A** again, sc2tog over last 2 sts, turn—46 sts.

ROW 4: Ch 1, sc in each st across, turn.

ROW 5: Ch 1, sk first st, work Row 5 of **Cable Charts A, B** and **A** again to last 2 sts of row, sc2tog over last 2 sts, turn—44 sts.

ROW 6: Work as Row 2—42 sts.

ROW 7: Ch 1, sk first st, sc in next 3 sts, FPdc around ea of next 4 FP sts, sc in next 5 sts, work Row 7 of **Cable Chart B,** sc in next 5 sts, FPdc around ea of next 4 FP sts, sc in next 2 sts, sc2tog over last 2 sts, turn—40 sts.

ROW 8: Work as Row 4.

ROW 9: Ch 1, sk first st, sc in next st,

FPdc around ea of next 2 FP sts, sc in next 2 sts, FPdc around next 2 sts, sc in next 4 sts, work Row 9 of **Cable Chart B,** sc in next 4 sts, FPdc around each of next 2 FP sts, sc in next 2 sts, FPdc around ea of next 2 FP sts, sc2tog over last 2 sts, turn—38 sts.

ROW 10: Work as Row 2—36 sts.

ROW 11: Ch 1, sk first st, sc in next 4 sts, FPdc around each of next 2 FP sts, sc in next 3 sts, work Row 11 of **Cable Chart B,** sc in next 3 sts, FPdc around each of next 2 FP sts, sc in next 3 sts, sc2tog over last 2 sts, turn—34 sts.

ROW 12: Work as Row 4.

ROW 13: Ch 1, sk first st, sc in next 4 sts, FPdc around ea of next 2 FP sts, sc in next 2 sts, work Row 13 of **Cable Chart B,** sc in next 2 sts, FPdc around ea of next 2 FP sts, sc in next 3 sts, sc2tog over last 2 sts, turn—32 sts.

ROW 14: Work as Row 2—30 sts.

ROW 15: Ch 1, sk first st, sc in next st, FPdc around ea of next 2 FP sts, sc in next 3 sts, work Row 1 of **Cable Chart B,** sc in next 3 sts, FPdc around ea of next 2 FP sts, sc2tog over last 2 sts, turn—28 sts.

ROW 16: Work as Row 4.

ROW 17: Ch 1, sk first st, sc in next 5 sts, work Row 3 of **Cable Chart B,** sc in next 4 sts, sc2tog over last 2 sts, turn—26 sts.

ROW 18: Work as Row 2—24 sts.

ROW 19: Ch 1, sk first st, sc in next 3 sts, work Row 5 of **Cable Chart B,** sc in next 2 sts, sc2tog—22 sts.

Fasten off.

ROW 3: Ch 1, sk first st, sc in next 3 sts, work Row 5 of **Cable Chart A, B,** and **A** again, sc in next 2 sts, sc2tog over last 2 sts, turn—50 sts.

ROW 4: Ch 1, sc in ea st across, turn.

ROW 5: Ch 1, sk first st, sc in next 2 sts, work Row 7 of **Cable Chart A, B,** and **A** again, sc in next st, sc2tog over last 2 sts, turn—48 sts.

ROW 6: Work as Row 2—46 sts.

ROW 7: Ch 1, sk first st, work Row 9 of **Cable Chart A, B,** and **A** again to last 2 sts of row, sc2tog—44 sts.

ROW 8: Work as Row 4.

ROW 9: Ch 1, sk first st, sc in next 2 sts, FPdc around ea of next 2 FP sts, sc in next 4 sts, FPdc around ea of next 2 FP sts, sc in next 3 sts, work Row 11 of **Cable Chart B,** sc in next 3 sts, FPdc around ea of next 2 FP sts, sc in next 4 sts, FPdc around ea of next 2 FP sts, sc in next st, sc2tog over last 2 sts, turn—42 sts.

ROW 10: Work as Row 2—40 sts.

ROW 11: Ch 1, sk first st, sc in next 7 sts, FPdc around ea of next 2 FP sts, sc in next 2 sts, work Row 13 of **Cable Chart B,** sc in next 2 sts, FPdc around ea of next 2 FP sts, sc in next 6 sts, sc2tog over last 2 sts, turn—38 sts.

ROW 12: Work as Row 4.

ROW 13: Ch 1, sk first st, sc in next 5 sts, FPdc around ea of next 2 FP sts, sc in next 3 sts, work Row 1 of **Cable Chart B,** sc in next 3 sts, FPdc around ea of next 2 FP sts, sc in next 4 sts, sc2tog over last 2 sts, turn—36 sts.

ROW 14: Work as Row 2—34 sts.

ROW 15: Ch 1, sk first st, sc in next 2 sts, FPdc around ea of next 2 FP sts, sc in next 4 sts, work Row 3 of **Cable Chart B,** sc in next 4 sts, FPdc around ea of next 2 FP sts, sc in next st, sc2tog over last 2 sts, turn—32 sts.

ROW 16: Work as Row 2—30 sts.

ROW 17: Ch 1, sk first st, sc in next 6 sts, work Row 5 of **Cable Chart B,** sc in next 5 sts, sc2tog over last 2 sts, turn—28 sts.

ROW 18: Work as Row 2—26 sts.

ROW 19: Ch 1, sk first st, sc in next 4 sts, work Row 7 of **Cable Chart B,** sc in next 3 sts, sc2tog over last 2 sts, turn—24 sts.

ROW 20: Work as Row 2—22 sts.

Fasten off.

Right Front

Ch 11 (12, 13, 14).

ROW 1 (RS): Sc in 2nd ch from hook and in ea ch across—10 (11, 12, 13) sts.

ROW 2 AND ALL EVEN ROWS UNTIL OTHERWISE STATED: Ch 1, sc in each st across, turn.

ROW 3: Ch 5, sc in 2nd ch from hook and in ea ch st, sc in next 4 (5) sts, FPdc in next 2 sts, sc in next 4 sts, turn—14 (15) sts.

ROW 3: Ch 5, sc in 2nd ch from hook and in ea ch st, FPdc in next 4 sts, sc in next 2 sts, FPdc in next 2 sts, sc in next 4 (5) sts, turn—16 (17) sts.

ALL SIZES:

ROW 5: Ch 3, sc in 2nd ch from hook and in next ch st, work Row 3 of **Cable Chart B,** beg with the 5th (4th, 3rd, 3rd) st of chart, sc in last 2 (2, 2, 3) sts, turn—16 (17, 18, 19) sts.

SIZES S, M ONLY:

ROW 7: Ch 2, sc in 2nd ch from hook, work Row 5 of **Cable Chart B,** beg with the 3rd (2nd) st of chart, sc in last 2 sts, turn—17 (18) sts.

SIZE L ONLY:

ROW 7: Ch 2, sc in 2nd ch from hook, work Row 5 of **Cable Chart B,** beg with the 1st st of chart, sc in last 2 sts, turn—19 sts.

SIZE XL ONLY:

ROW 7: Ch 3, sc in 2nd ch from hook and in next ch st, work Row 5 of **Cable Chart B,** sc in last 3 sts, turn—21 sts.

ALL SIZES:

ROW 9: Ch 2, sc in 2nd ch from hook, sc in next 0 (0, 1, 2) sts, work Row 7 of **Cable Chart B,** beg with the 2nd (1st, 1st, 1st) st of chart, sc in last 2 (2, 2, 3) sts, turn—18 (19, 20, 22) sts.

ROW 11: Ch 2, sc in 2nd ch from hook, sc in next 0 (1, 2, 3) sts, work Row 9 of **Cable Chart B,** sc in last 2 (2, 2, 3) sts, turn—19 (20, 21, 23) sts.

ROW 12: Ch 1, sc in ea st across, turn.

Continue working without increasing as follows:

ALL EVEN ROWS: Ch 1, sc in ea st across, turn.

ALL UNEVEN ROWS: Ch 1, sc in first 1 (2, 3, 4) sts, work **Cable Chart B,** sc in last 2 (2, 2, 3) sts, turn.

Starting with Row 13, work even in patt for 14 (16, 18, 20) rows, ending with Row 10 (12, 14, 2) of **Cable Chart B.**

Start Raglan Decreases

ROW 1: Ch 1, sc in next 1 (2, 3, 4) sts, work Row 11 (13, 1, 3) of **Cable Chart B,** sc in next 0 (0, 0, 1) sc, sc2tog over last 2 sts, turn—18 (19, 20, 22) sts.

ROW 2: Ch 1, sk first st, sc in each st across, turn—17 (18, 19, 21) sts.

ROW 3: Ch 1, sc in next 1 (2, 3, 4) sts, work first 14 (14, 14, 15) sts of Row 13 (1, 3, 5) of **Cable Chart B,** sc2tog over last 2 sts, turn—16 (17, 18, 20) sts.

ROW 4: Ch 1, sc in each st across, turn.

ROW 5: Ch 1, sc in first 1 (2, 3, 4) sts,

work first 13 (13, 12, 14) sts of Row 1 (3, 5, 7) of Cable Chart B, sc in next 0 (0, 1, 0) st, sc2tog over last 2 sts, turn—15 (16, 17, 19) sts.

ROW 6: Work as Row 2—14 (15, 16, 18) sts.

ROW 7: Ch 1, sc in first 1 (2, 3, 4) sts, work first 11 (11, 11, 12) sts of Row 3 (5, 7, 9) of **Cable Chart B,** sc2tog over last 2 sts, turn—13 (14, 15, 17) sts.

ROW 8: Work as Row 4.

ROW 9: Ch 1, sc in first 1 (2, 3, 4) sts, work first 10 (10, 10, 9) sts of Row 5 (7, 9, 11) of **Cable Chart B,** sc in next 0 (0, 0, 2) sts, sc2tog over last 2 sts, turn—12 (13, 14, 16) sts.

ROW 10: Work as Row 2—11 (12, 13, 15) sts.

ROW 11: Ch 1, sc in first 1 (2, 3, 4) sts, work first 8 sts of Row 7 (9, 11, 13) of **Cable Chart B,** sc in next 0 (0, 0, 1) sts, sc2tog over last 2 sts, turn—10 (11, 12, 14) sts.

SIZES M, L, XL ONLY:

ROW 12: Work as Row 4.

SIZES L, XL ONLY:

ROW 13: Ch 1, sc in next 3 (4) sts, work first 7 (4) sts of Row 13 (1) of **Cable Chart B,** sc in next 0 (4) sts, sc2tog over last 2 sts, turn—11 (13) sts.

SIZE XL ONLY:

ROW 14: Work as Row 2—12 sts.

Start Neckline

SIZES S, M ONLY:

ROW 1: Ch 1, sc in first 8 sts, turn, leaving rem sts unworked—8 sts.

SIZES M, XL ONLY:

ROW 1: Ch 1, sk first st, sl st in next st, sc in next 0 (2) sts, work first 7 (4) sts of Row 11 (3) of **Cable Chart B,** sc in next 0 (2) sts, sc2tog over last 2 sts, turn, leaving rem sts unworked—8 (9) sts.

SIZES S, M, XL ONLY:

ROW 2: Ch 1, sk first st, sc in next 5 (5, 6) sts, sc2tog over last 2 sts, turn—6 (6, 7) sts.

SIZE L ONLY:

ROW 2: Ch 1, sk first st, sc in next st, FPdc around ea of next 2 FP sts, sc in next 2 sts, sc2tog over last 2 sts, turn, leaving rem sts unworked—6 sts.

ROW 3: Ch 1, sc in first 4 sts, sc2tog over last 2 sts, turn—5 sts.

SIZES S, M, XL ONLY:

ROW 3: Ch 1, sk first st, sc in next 3 (3, 4) sts, sc2tog over last 2 sts, turn—4 (4, 5) sts.

SIZE S ONLY:

ROW 4: Ch 1, sc in first 2 sts, sc2tog over last 2 sts, turn—3 sts.

SIZE M ONLY:

ROW 4: Ch 1, sc in ea st across, turn.

SIZE L ONLY:

ROW 4: Ch 1, sc in first st, FPdc around ea of next 2 FP sts, sc2tog over last 2 sts, turn—4 sts.

SIZE XL ONLY:

ROW 4: Ch 1, sk first st, sc in next 2 sts, sc2tog over last 2 sts, turn—3 sts.

SIZES S, XL ONLY:

ROW 5: Ch 1, sc in first st, sc2tog over last 2 sts, turn—2 sts.

SIZES M, L ONLY:

ROW 5: Ch 1, sk first st, sc in next st, sc2tog over last 2 sts, turn—2 sts.

ALL SIZES:

ROW 6: Ch 1, sc2tog—1 st.

Fasten off.

Left Front

Ch 11 (12, 13, 14).

ROW 1 (RS): Sc in 2nd ch from hook and in ea ch across—10 (11, 12, 13) sts.

ROW 2: Ch 1, sc in ea st across, turn.

ROW 3: Ch 1, sc in first 2 (2, 2, 3) sts, work first 6 (6, 10, 10) sts of Row 1 of **Cable Chart B,** sc in next 2 (3, 0, 0) sts, turn.

ROW 4: Ch 5, sc in 2nd ch from hook and in ea ch and st across, turn—14 (15, 16, 17) sts.

ROW 5: Ch 1, sc in first 2 (2, 2, 3) sts, work first 12 (12, 14, 14) sts of Row 3 of **Cable Chart B,** sc in next 0 (1, 0, 0) st, turn.

ROW 6: Ch 3, sc in 2nd ch from hook and in ea ch and st across, turn—16 (17, 18, 19) sts.

ROW 7: Ch 1, sc in first 2 (2, 2, 3) sts, work first 14 sts of Row 5 of **Cable Chart B,** sc in next 0 (1, 2, 2) sts, turn.

ROW 8: Ch 2 (2, 2, 3), sc in 2nd ch from hook and in ea ch and st across, turn—17 (18, 19, 21) sts.

SIZE S ONLY:

ROW 9: Ch 1, sc in first 2 sts, work first 15 sts of Row 7 of **Cable Chart B,** turn.

SIZES M, L, XL ONLY:

ROW 9: Ch 1, sc in first 2 (2, 3) sts, work Row 7 of **Cable Chart B,** sc in next 0 (1, 2) sts, turn.

ALL SIZES:

ROW 10: Ch 2, sc in 2nd ch from hook and in ea st across, turn—18 (19, 20, 22) sts.

ROW 11: Ch 1, sc in first 2 (2, 2, 3) sts, work Row 9 of **Cable Chart B,** sc in next 0 (1, 2, 3) sts, turn.

ROW 12: Ch 2, sc in 2nd ch from hook and in ea st across, turn—19 (20, 21, 23) sts.

Cont working without increasing as foll:

ALL UNEVEN ROWS: Ch 1, sc in first 2 (2, 2, 3) sts, work **Cable Chart B,** sc in next 1 (2, 3, 4) sts, turn.

ALL EVEN ROWS: Ch 1, sc in ea st across, turn.

Starting with Row 13 of **Cable Chart B,** work even in patt for 14 (16, 18, 20) rows, ending with Row 10 (12, 14, 2) of **Cable Chart B.**

Start Raglan Decreases

ROW 1: Ch 1, sk first st, sc in next 1 (1, 1, 2) sts, work Row 11 (13, 1, 3) of **Cable Chart B,** sc in last 1 (2, 3, 4) sts, turn—18 (19, 20, 22) sts.

ROW 2: Ch 1, sc in ea st across to last 2 sts, sc2tog over last 2 sts, turn—17 (18, 19, 21) sts.

ROW 3: Ch 1, sk first st, work Row 13 (1, 3, 5) of **Cable Chart B,** beg with 2nd (2nd, 2nd, 1st) st of chart, sc in last 1 (2, 3, 4) sts, turn—16 (17, 18, 20) sts.

ROW 4: Ch 1, sc in each st across, turn.

ROW 5: Ch 1, sk first st, sc in next 4 (4, 4, 0) sts, work Row 1 (3, 5, 7) of **Cable Chart B,** beg with 7th (7th, 7th 2nd) st of chart (patt beg: 4 FPdc [4-st-dc-cable, 4 FPdc, sc]), sc in last 1 (2, 3, 4) sts, turn—15 (16, 17, 19) sts.

ROW 6: Work as Row 2—14 (15, 16, 18) sts.

ROW 7: Ch 1, sk first st, sc in next 2 sts, work Row 3 (5, 7, 9) of **Cable Chart B,** beg with 7th (7th 7th 6th) st of chart (patt beg: dc-cable [4 FPdc, dc-cable, 2 FPdc]), sc in last 1 (2, 3, 4) sts, turn—13 (14, 15, 17) sts.

ROW 8: Work as Row 4.

ROW 9: Ch 1, sk first st, sc in next 1 (1, 4, 5) sts, work Row 5 (7, 9, 11) of **Cable Chart B,** beg with 7th (7th, 10th, 10th) st of chart (patt beg: 4 FPdc [dc-cable, 4 FPdc, 2nd tr-cable-front]), sc in last 1 (2, 3, 4) sts, turn—12 (13, 14, 16) sts.

ROW 10: Work as Row 2—11 (12, 13, 15) sts.

ROW 11: Ch 1, sk first st, sc in next 1 (2, 2, 2) sts, work Row 7 (9, 11, 13) of **Cable Chart B,** beg with 9th (10th, 10th 9th) st of chart (patt beg: 2nd half of dc-cable, 4 FPdc, 2nd tr-cable-front, 2 FPdc), sc in last 1 (2, 3, 4) sts, turn—10 (11, 12, 14) sts.

SIZES M, L, XL ONLY:

ROW 12: Work as Row 4.

SIZES L, XL ONLY:

ROW 13: Ch 1, sk first st, sc in next 4 (5) sts, FPdc around ea of next 2 FP sts, sc in last 5 (6) sts, turn—11 (13) sts.

SIZE XL ONLY:

ROW 14: Work as Row 2—12 sts.

Start Neckline

SIZE S ONLY:

ROW 1: Ch 1, sk first st, sl st in next st, sc in next 8 sts, turn, leaving rem st unworked—8 sts.

SIZE M ONLY:

ROW 1: Ch 1, sk first st, sc in next st, work Row 11 of **Cable Chart B,** beg with 10th st of chart (work 2nd tr-cable-front and following 2 sc), sc2tog over last 2 sts, turn—8 sts.

SIZE L ONLY:

ROW 1: Ch 1, sk first st, sl st in next st, sc in ea st across to last 2 sts, sc2tog over last 2 sts, turn—8 sts.

SIZE XL ONLY:

ROW 1: Ch 1, sk first st, sc in next 3 sts, FPdc around ea of next 2 FP sts, sc in next 3 sts, sc2tog over last 2 sts, turn, leaving rem sts unworked—9 sts.

SIZES S, M, XL ONLY:

ROW 2: Ch 1, sk first st, sc in next 5 (5, 6) sts, sc2tog over last 2 sts, turn—6 (6, 7) sts.

ROW 3: Ch 1, sk first st, sc in next 3 (3, 4) sts, sc2tog over last 2 sts, turn—4 (4, 5) sts.

SIZE L ONLY:

ROW 2: Ch 1, sk first st, sc in next 2 sts, FPdc around each of next 2 FP sts, sc in next st, sc2tog over last 2 sts, turn—6 sts.

ROW 3: Ch 1, sk first st, sc in each st across, turn—5 sts.

ROW 4: Ch 1, sk first st, sc in next st, FPdc around ea of next 2 FP sts, sc in last st, turn—4 sts.

SIZES S, M ONLY:

ROW 4: Ch 1, sk first st, sc in ea st across, turn—3 (3) sts.

SIZE XL ONLY:

ROW 4: Ch 1, sk first st, sc in next 2 sts, sc2tog over last 2 sts, turn—3 sts.

SIZE S, M, XL ONLY:

ROW 5: Ch 1, sk first st, sc in each st across, turn—2 (2, 2) sts.

SIZE L ONLY:

ROW 5: Ch 1, sk first st, sc in next st, sc2tog over last 2 sts, turn—2 sts.

ALL SIZES:

ROW 6: Ch 1, sc2tog—1 st.

Fasten off.

Sleeves

Ch 29 (31, 31, 31).

ROW 1 (RS): Sc in 2nd ch from hook and in ea ch across, turn—28 (30, 30, 30) sc.

ROW 2 AND ALL EVEN ROWS: Ch 1, sc in ea st across, turn.

ROW 3: Ch 1, sc in next 6 (7, 7, 7) sts, work Row 1 of **Cable Chart B,** sc in last 6 (7, 7, 7) sts, turn.

ROW 5 (INC ROW): Ch 1, 2 sc in first st, sc in next 5 (6, 6, 6) sts, work Row 3 of **Cable Chart B,** sc in next 5 (6, 6, 6) sts, 2 sc in last st—30 (32, 32, 32) sts.

Cont working cable pattern over the center 16 sts, following **Cable Chart B,** working sc on either side of center 16 st.

ROWS 6-24 (28, 30, 32): Inc 1 sc at each end of every 4th row (2 [0, 2, 4] times); then inc 1 sc at each end of every 6th row (1 [3, 2, 1] times)—36 (38, 40, 42) sts; then work 5 rows even in patt, ending with Row 8 (12, 14, 2) of **Cable Chart B.**

Start Raglan Decreases

ROW 1: Ch 1, sk first st (dec made), sc in next 11 (12, 13, 14) sts, work center 12 sts of Row 9 (13, 1, 3) of **Cable Chart B,**

sc in next 10 (11, 12, 13) sts, sc2tog (dec made), turn—34 (36, 38, 40) sts.

ROW 2: Ch 1, sk first st (dec made), sc across to last 2 sts, sc2tog (dec made)—32 (34, 36, 38) sts.

ROWS 3–16 (18, 19, 20): Maintaining est patt, working center 12 sts following center 12 sts on **Cable Chart B,** dec 1 st at each end of next row, *work 1 row even, dec 1 st at each end of next 3 rows; rep from * 2 (2, 2, 3) times, work 1 row even, dec 1 st at each end of next 1 (2, 2, 0) rows. Work 1 (0, 1, 1) row even—12 (10, 12, 12) sts. Sizes M, L, XL only: Fasten off.

SIZE S ONLY:

ROW 17: Ch 1, sk first st, sc in next 2 sts, FPdc 2 around each of 1st and 2nd FP sts 2 rows below, sc in next 2 sts, FPdc around each of last 2 FP sts 2 rows below, sc in next st, sc2tog over last 2 sts, turn—10 sts.

Fasten off.

Finishing

Block all pieces to finished measurements (see Schematics on page 104). With RS facing, whipstitch side and sleeve seams, sew raglan seams.

Neck Edging

With RS facing, join yarn to top of right front neck edge, ch 11.

ROW 1: Sc in 2nd ch from hook and in ea ch across, sl st to fabric twice (first sl st joins ribbing to body, second counts as a tch), turn—10 sc.

ROW 2: Sk both sl sts, sc-blo in each sc across, turn.

ROW 3: Ch 1, sc-blo in each sc across, turn.

Rep Rows 2–3 evenly around neck. End with a WS row, do not fasten off.

Body Edging

Turn work, RS facing, in order to work edging down the Left Front.

ROW 1: Ch 11, sc in 2nd ch from hook and in ea ch across, sl st to fabric twice, turn—10 sc.

ROW 2: Sk both sl sts, sc-blo in each sc across, turn.

ROW 3: Ch 1, sc-blo in each sc across, turn.

Rep Rows 2–3 evenly down Left Front, around lower back and back up Right Front, ending with a WS row. Fasten off.

Cuff Edging

With RS facing, join yarn to cuff at sleeve seam, ch 11.

ROW 1: Sc in 2nd ch from hook and in ea ch across, sl st to fabric twice, turn—10 sc.

ROW 2: Sk both sl sts, sc-blo in each sc across, turn.

ROW 3: Ch 1, sc-blo in each sc across, turn.

Rep Rows 2–3 evenly around wrist, ending with a WS row, do not fasten off. Turn cuff inside out. Put loop back on hook, with foundation ch and last row held together, sl st across working through both layers. Fasten off.

Block cardigan again, including Edgings.

Place a marker ½" (1.3 cm) below neck edge on RS of Left Front. Place 2nd marker 4½ (4¾, 5, 5¼)" (11.5 [12, 12.5, 13.5] cm) below first marker and place 3rd marker halfway between. Rep on WS of Right Front edge. Sew female halves of 3 snaps to RS of left front edge at markers, ½" (1.3 cm) in from edge. Sew male halves to WS of right front edge at markers, ½" (1.3 cm) in from edge.

Julia Vaconsin started designing in 2008 and has been published in *Interweave Crochet* as well as *Yarn Forward* and *Inside Crochet*. She sells some of her designs directly on her website, juliavaconsin.com, and on Ravelry.com. She is thrilled to be included as a contributor in her first book project.

If you had only one ball of yarn… I have a tendency to let special yarn sit on a shelf for too long, admiring it and waiting for that special idea that might never come, so I have to force myself to just make something with it. Recently, I made a wonderful lightweight shawl out of SweetGeorgia merino silk, which I bought directly from Felicia Lo's (aka SweetGeorgia) dye studio in Vancouver, B.C. The shawl reminds me of that wonderful trip to Vancouver whenever I wear it.

float vest and float cardigan

robyn chachula

I love wearing shawls—until I need to run errands. I've never quite been able to carry my huge purse while wearing a shawl without getting all tangled up! This vest solves that problem, while still providing the comfort of being wrapped in a cozy shawl. The armholes give you freedom of movement and the loose lower portion can be worn open or wrapped around and belted. You can even add sleeves quickly and easily for a different look.

MATERIALS

yarn: DK weight (#3 Light).

Shown: Brown Sheep Company, Cotton Fleece (80% cotton, 20% Merino wool; 215 yd [197 m]/3.5 oz [100 g]): CW460 jungle green (Vest), 4 (5, 5, 6, 7) balls; CW112 vintage linen (Cardigan), 6 (7, 7, 8, 9) balls.

hook: H/8 (5.0 mm) or hook needed to obtain gauge.

notions: Tapestry needle for weaving in ends; spray bottle with water and straight pins for blocking.

GAUGE

2 SR = 4⅜" (11.25 cm) 8 rows = 4⅜" (11.3 cm) in stitch pattern.

14 edc by 7 rows = 4" × 4" (10 × 10 cm) in edc rows.

FINISHED SIZE

S (M, L, XL, 2XL) Vest/Cardigan is sized to fit 32 (36, 40, 44, 48)" (81.5 [91.5, 101.5, 112, 122] cm) with a relaxed fit. Sample shown is a size M.

finished bust: 41½ (48, 54¾, 59, 68)" (105.5 [122, 139, 150, 172.5] cm).

finished length: 23¾ (23¾, 26, 27, 28¼)" (60.5 [60.5, 66, 69, 71.5] cm).

{notes}

* Vest is crocheted in one piece.

* To make the cardigan, simply follow the instructions to add sleeves to the vest. Refer to the Materials list at left for yarn requirements for the cardigan.

schematics

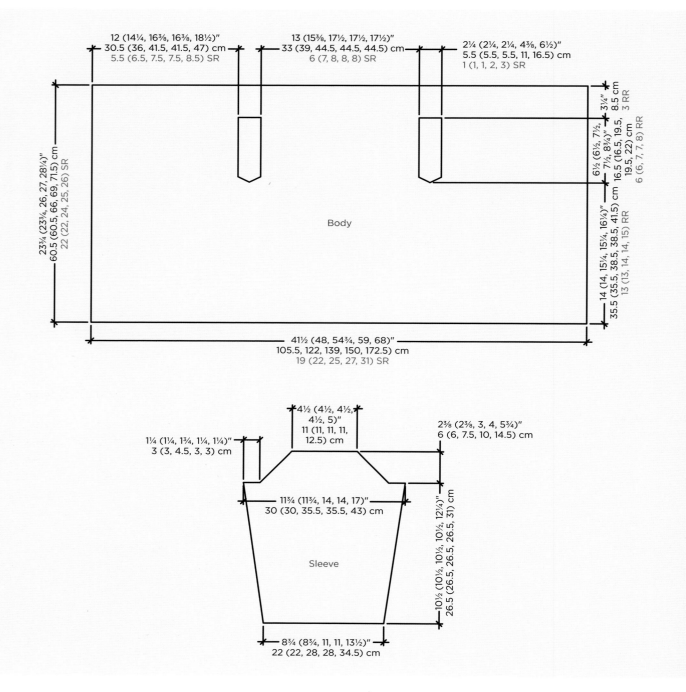

12 (14¼, 16⅜, 16⅜, 18½)"
30.5 (36, 41.5, 41.5, 47) cm
5.5 (6.5, 7.5, 7.5, 8.5) SR

13 (15⅜, 17½, 17½, 17½)"
33 (39, 44.5, 44.5, 44.5) cm
6 (7, 8, 8, 8) SR

2¼ (2¼, 2¼, 4⅜, 6½)"
5.5 (5.5, 5.5, 11, 16.5) cm
1 (1, 1, 2, 3) SR

3¼"
8.5 cm
3 RR

6½ (6½, 7½,
7½, 8¾)"
16.5 (16.5, 19.5,
19.5, 22) cm
6 (6, 7, 7, 8) RR

23¾ (23¾, 26, 27, 28¼)"
60.5 (60.5, 66, 69, 71.5) cm
22 (22, 24, 25, 26) SR

Body

14 (14, 15¼, 15¼, 16¼)"
35.5 (35.5, 38.5, 38.5, 41.5) cm
13 (13, 14, 14, 15) RR

41½ (48, 54¾, 59, 68)"
105.5, 122, 139, 150, 172.5) cm
19 (22, 25, 27, 31) SR

4½ (4½, 4½,
4½, 5)"
11 (11, 11, 11,
12.5) cm

2⅜ (2⅜, 3, 4, 5¾)"
6 (6, 7.5, 10, 14.5) cm

1¼ (1¼, 1¾, 1¼, 1¼)"
3 (3, 4.5, 3, 3) cm

11¾ (11¾, 14, 14, 17)"
30 (30, 35.5, 35.5, 43) cm

10½ (10½, 10½, 10½, 12¼)"
26.5 (26.5, 26.5, 26.5, 31) cm

Sleeve

8¾ (8¾, 11, 11, 13½)"
22 (22, 28, 28, 34.5) cm

details

Special Stitches

V Stitch (v-st): (Dc, ch 1, dc) in st indicated.

Trefoil: (Ch 3, [sc, ch 3] 3 times, sc, ch 3) in st indicated.

Extended Double Crochet (edc): Yo, insert hook into st indicated, yo, pull up lp, yo, draw through one lp on hook, yo, draw through 2 lps on hook, yo, draw through 2 lps on hook.

Trefoil Stitch Pattern (tsp)

Refer to the **Trefoil Stitch Pattern** diagram at right for assistance.

Ch 34.

ROW 1 (RS): Dc in 4th ch from hook, *sk 4 ch, trefoil in next ch, sk 4 ch, v-st in next ch; rep from * to last 10 ch, sk 4 ch, trefoil in next ch, sk 4 ch, 2 dc in last ch, turn—3 trefoils.

ROW 2: Ch 4 (counts as dc, ch-1 sp), [sc, ch 3] twice in first dc, sk next 2 ch-3 sps, v-st in next ch-3 sp, *trefoil in next ch-1 sp, sk next 2 ch-3 sps, v-st in next ch-3 sp; rep from * to last trefoil, ch 3, [sc, ch 3, sc, ch 1, dc] in top of tch, turn.

ROW 3: Ch 3 (counts as dc), dc in first dc, *sk next 2 ch-3 sps, trefoil in next ch-1 sp, sk next 2 ch-3 sps, v-st in next ch-3 sp; rep from * to last trefoil, trefoil in next ch-1 sp, sk next 2 ch-3 sps, 2 dc in 3rd ch of tch, turn.

Rep Rows 2–3 to desired length.

LAST ROW: Ch 1, sc in first dc, *ch 4, sk next 2 ch-3 sp, sc in next ch-1 sp, ch 4, sk next 2 ch-3 sp, sc in next ch-4 sp; rep from * across to last trefoil, ch 4, sc in 3rd ch of tch, turn.

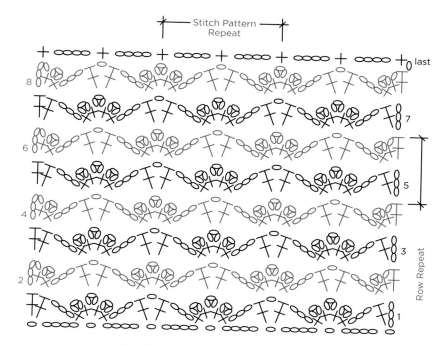

Trefoil Stitch Pattern Diagram

pattern

Body

Ch 194 (224, 254, 274, 314)

ROW 1 (RS): Dc in 4th ch from hook, *sk 4 ch, trefoil in next ch, sk 4 ch, v-st in next ch; rep from * to last 10 ch, sk 4 ch, trefoil in next ch, sk 4 ch, 2 dc in last ch, turn—19 (22, 25, 27, 31) trefoils.

Rep Rows 2–3 of tsp 12 (12, 13, 13, 14) times; rep Row 2 once.

Refer to **Stitch Diagram A** on page 118 for assistance with armhole shaping.

Right Front Armhole Shaping

ROW 1: Work in Row 3 of tsp for 6 (7, 8, 8, 9) trefoils, ch 3, sk next 2 ch-3 sps, dc in next ch-3 sp, turn.

ROW 2: Ch 4, sk next 2 ch-3 sps, v-st in next ch-3 sp, cont in Row 2 of tsp across to end, turn—5 (6, 7, 7, 8) trefoils.

ROW 3: Work in Row 3 of tsp to last trefoil, v-st in last trefoil, ch 3, [sc, ch 3, sc, ch 1, dc] in last ch-1 sp, turn.

ROW 4: Ch 3 (counts as dc), dc in first dc, cont in Row 3 of tsp to last trefoil, v-st in last trefoil, ch 3, [sc, ch 3, sc, ch 1, dc] in top of tch, turn.

Rep Row 4 eight (eight, ten, twelve, twelve) times. Fasten off. Weave in ends.

Back Armhole Shaping

ROW 1: With RS facing, join with sl st in middle ch-3 sp of same trefoil (same trefoil, same trefoil, 1 trefoil to the left, 2 trefoils to the left) of Right Front, ch 6 (counts as dc, ch-3 sp), cont in Row 3 of tsp for 7 (8, 9, 9, 9) trefoils, ch 3, sk next 2 ch-3 sps, dc in next ch-3 sp, turn.

ROW 2: Ch 4, sk next 2 ch-3 sps, v-st in next ch-3 sp, cont in Row 2 of tsp across to last trefoil, v-st in last trefoil, tr in 3rd ch of tch, turn—6 (7, 8, 8, 8) trefoils.

ROW 3: Sl st in next 3 sts, ch 4 (counts as dc, ch-1 sp), [sc, ch 3] twice in first ch-1 sp, sk next 2 ch-3 sps, v-st in next ch-3 sp, cont in Row 3 of tsp to last trefoil, v-st in last trefoil, ch 3, [sc, ch 3, sc, ch 1, dc] in last ch-1 sp, turn—5 (6, 7, 7, 7) trefoils plus one half trefoil at ea end of row.

ROW 4: Rep Row 3 of tsp, turn.

ROW 5: Rep Row 2 of tsp, turn.

Rep Rows 4–5 three (three, four, five, five) times, then rep Row 4 once, ch 9 (9, 9, 19, 29), sl st to top of tch of last row of armhole shaping on Right Front. Fasten off. Weave in ends.

Left Front Armhole Shaping

ROW 1: With RS facing, join with sl st to middle ch-3 sp of same trefoil (same trefoil, same trefoil, 1 trefoil to the left, 2 trefoils to the left) of Back, ch 6 (counts as dc, ch-3 sp), cont in Row 3 of tsp for 6 (7, 8, 8, 9) trefoils, ch 3, sk

A. Armhole Shaping

next 2 ch-3 sps, 2 dc in last ch-sp, turn.

ROW 2: Ch 4, [sc, ch 3] twice in first dc, sk next 2 ch-3 sps, v-st in next ch-3 sp, cont in Row 2 of tsp across to last trefoil, v-st in last trefoil, tr in 3rd ch of tch, turn—5 (6, 7, 7, 8) trefoils.

ROW 3: Sl st in next 3 sts, ch 4 (counts as dc, ch-1 sp), [sc, ch 3] twice in first ch-1 sp, sk next 2 ch-3 sps, v-st in next ch-3 sp, cont in Row 3 of tsp to end, turn—5 (6, 7, 7, 9) trefoils.

ROW 4: Ch 4 (counts as dc, ch-1 sp), [sc, ch 3] twice in first dc, sk next 2 ch-3 sps, v-st in next ch-3 sp, cont in Row 3 of tsp to end, turn.

Rep Row 4 eight (eight, ten, twelve, twelve) times, ch 9 (9, 9, 19, 29), sl st to top of tch of last row of armhole shaping on Back. Fasten off. Weave in ends.

Collar

ROW 1: With RS facing, join yarn in first st on last row of First Front, ch 3, dc in first dc, *cont in Row 3 of tsp to armhole opening, trefoil in top of tch, sk 4 ch, v-st in next ch, [sk 4 ch, trefoil in next ch, sk 4 ch, v-st in next ch] 0 (0, 0, 1, 2) times, sk 4 ch, trefoil in next dc; rep from * once, cont in Row 3 of tsp across to end, turn—19 (22, 25, 27, 31) trefoils.

Rep Rows 2–3 of tsp twice; rep Row 2 once.

stitch *matters*

Not all stitches are created equal. Have you ever noticed that sweaters with tall stitches, like double or treble crochet, usually drape and flow easier than single crochet sweaters? The reason for this is actually quite simple. Those little squat stitches, like single crochet, use more yarn than their taller counterparts.

So why do those taller stitches use less yarn? Well, think about how the single crochet stitch is made. You insert your hook into the row below and yarn over, making a very short stitch. Though the treble crochet also has to pass through the row below and come up; on all the rest of the yarn overs, it only has to pull through loops on the hook and does not go through the row again. That little extra yarn you need to go through the row with the shorter stitches really starts to add up. Another way of thinking about it is to consider the amount of "air" between the stitches. Single crochet stitches are so short and squat and crammed together that they have little space between the stitches, while treble crochet stitches are long and lean and have lots of space. The more space or "air" in the fabric, the less yarn you will need.

Now, how can you use this information to your advantage? When choosing a stitch pattern to use, keep in mind the airiness of the stitches. Lacy stitches tend to use the least yarn, while cables tend to use the most. If you have your eye on some beautiful but expensive yarn, look around for a project that uses a lacy stitch pattern or tall stitches to get a lot of bang for your buck. On the other hand, if you really have you heart set on creating some fabulous cables or you've fallen in love with a dense stitch pattern, go with a less expensive yarn or try making smaller projects, such as a scarf or a hat.

Robyn Chachula

ROW 7: Ch 1, sc in first dc, *ch 4, sc in next ch-1 sp, ch 4, sk 2 ch-3 sps**, sc in next ch-3 sp; rep from * across, ending last rep at **, sc in top of tch. Fasten off. Weave in ends.

Blocking and Edging

Pin Body to finished measurements (refer to Schematics on page 116), spray with water and allow to dry. Join yarn to RS of armhole, ch 1, sc evenly around, sl st to first sc, fasten off. Weave in ends.

Body Edging

ROW 1: Join yarn to RS back, ch 1, sc evenly around body, placing 3 sc on all outside corners, do not turn, join with sl st in first sc.

ROW 2: Ch 4 (counts as edc), edc in ea sc around, placing 5 edc in middle sc on outside corners, do not turn, join with sl st in top of t-ch.

ROW 3: Ch 1, sc bet ea edc around, sl st to first sc. Fasten off. Weave in ends.

Sleeve for Cardigan

Make 2.

Ch 32 (32, 40, 40, 48).

ROW 1 (RS): Dc in 4th ch from hook (sk ch count as dc), dc in ea rem ch across, turn—30 (30, 38, 38, 46) dc.

ROW 2: Ch 3, edc bet ea 2 sts across, turn.

ROW 3 (INC ROW): Ch 3 (counts as dc), 2 edc bet first 2 sts, edc bet ea 2 sts across to last, 2 edc bet last 2 sts, turn—32 (32, 40, 40, 48) sts.

*Rep Row 2 twice, rep Row 3, rep from * 3 (3, 3, 3, 4) times. Rep Row 2 three times—40 (40, 48, 48, 58) sts.

Cap Shaping

XL, 2XL ONLY:

ROW 1: Sl st in next 4 sts, ch 3 (counts as dc), edc bet ea 2 sts across to last 4 sts, leave rem sts unworked, turn—39 (49) sts.

2XL ONLY:

ROW 2: Ch 3, edc bet ea 2 sts across, turn.

XL, 2XL:

ROW 2 (3): Ch 1, sc bet first 2 sts, hdc bet next sts, edc bet ea 2 sts across to last 2 sts, hdc bet next 2 sts, sc bet last sts, sl st in last st, turn—35 (45) edc.

S, M, L ONLY:

ROW 1: Sl st in next 4 (4, 6) sts, sc bet next 2 sts, hdc bet next 2 sts, edc bet next 27 (27, 31) sts, hdc bet next 2 sts, sc bet next 2 sts, sl st in next st, turn—27 (27, 31) edc.

ALL SIZES:

ROW 2 (2, 2, 3, 4): Sk sl st, sl st in next sc, sl st in next hdc, sc bet next 2 sts, hdc bet next 2 sts, edc bet next 24 (24, 28, 32, 42) sts, hdc bet next sts, sc bet next sts, sl st in next st—23 (23, 27, 31, 41) edc.

Rep prev row twice (twice, 3 times, 4 times, 6 times) with 4 fewer edc on ea row—16 (16, 16, 16, 18) edc. Fasten off.

Pin sleeves to schematic size and spray with water to block. With right sides facing, pin sleeve to arm opening, whipstitch in place. Whipstitch underarm seam, turn right side out. Join yarn to edge of sleeve cuff, ch 1, sc evenly around cuff edge, join with sl st in first sc. Fasten off. Weave in ends.

annabel shawl

kristin omdahl

This gorgeous shawl is made up of simple 3-round motifs that create an interesting geometric pattern when joined together as a fabric. The unusual edging is an exciting part of making this shawl because it is worked back and forth in sections (like motifs), but with one continuous piece of yarn. I think you'll find the process of crocheting this piece both enjoyable and refreshing.

MATERIALS

yarn: Sportweight (#2 Fine).

Shown: Brown Sheep Company Nature Spun Sport Weight (100% wool; 184 yd [168 m]/1.75 oz [50 g]): #103 deep sea, 4 balls.

hook: D/3 (3.25 mm) or hook needed to obtain gauge.

notions: Tapestry needle for weaving in ends; spray bottle with water and straight pins for blocking.

GAUGE

1 finished motif (3 rounds) = 3½" × 3½" (9 × 9 cm).

FINISHED SIZE

52" across × 28" deep (132 × 71 cm).

{note}

* Work two rounds of motifs, then third round is worked to join motifs together. Follow Joining and Edging Diagram to join motifs together.

details

Special Stitches

2 Double Crochet Cluster (2dc-cl):
p. 155.

3 Double Crochet Cluster (3dc-cl):
p. 155.

Dc3tog worked over 7 sts: Yo, insert hook in next dc, yo, pull up a lp, yo, draw through 2 lps on hook, sk next 2 dc, yo, insert hook in next sc, yo, pull up a lp, yo, draw through 2 lps on hook, sk next 2 dc, yo, insert hook in next dc, yo, pull up a lp, yo, draw through 2 lps on hook, yo, draw yarn through 4 lps on hook.

pattern

Window Square Motif

Make 1, Join 63.

See **Stitch Diagram A** above right for assistance.

Ch 5, sl st to join in ring.

RND 1 (RS): Ch 2, work 2dc-cl in ring, *ch 7, 3dc-cl in ring; rep from * twice, ch 3, tr in beg st to join (counts as ch-7), do not turn.

RND 2: Ch 3 (counts as dc), work 3 dc around post of tr, sc in next 3dc-cl, *(4 dc, ch 3, 4 dc) in next ch-7 sp, sc in next 3dc-cl; rep from * twice, 4 dc in next ch-3 sp, ch 1, hdc in top of tch (counts as ch-3 sp), do not turn—12 dc.

RND 3: Ch 1, (sc, ch 7, sc) in same sp, *ch 7, work dc3tog over next 7 sts**, ch 7, (sc, ch 7, sc) in next ch-7 sp; rep from * twice. Rep from * to ** once more, ch 7, sl st in first sc to join. Fasten off.

Joining

Join motifs using **Stitch Diagram B** below. Join motifs in order listed.

Joining Motifs (2–15, 16, 29, 40, 49, 56, 61, 64)

Cont in directions for Window Square Motif to Rnd 3.

RND 3: Ch 1, (sc, ch 3, sl st in ch-7 sp on adjacent motif, ch 3, sc) in same sp, (ch 3, sl st in next ch-7 sp on adjacent motif, ch 3) work dc3tog over next 7 sts. Ch 3, sl st in next ch-7 sp on adjacent

A. Window Square Motif

B. Joining and Edging Diagram

motif, ch 3, in next ch-7 sp work (sc, ch 3, sl st in ch-7 sp on adjacent motif, ch 3, sc). *Ch 7, work dc3tog over next 7 sts**. Ch 7, (sc, ch 7, sc) in next ch-7 sp. Rep from * one more time. Rep from * to ** once more. Ch 7, sl st in sc at beg of round to join. Fasten off.

Joining Motifs (17–28, 30–39, 41–48, 50–55, 57–60, 62–63)

Cont in directions for Window Square Motif to Rnd 3.

RND 3: Ch 1, (sc, ch 3, sl st in ch-7 sp on adjacent motif, ch 3, sc) in same sp, [(ch 3, sl st in next ch-7 sp on adjacent motif, ch 3) work dc3tog over next 7 sts. Ch 3, sl st in next ch-7 sp on adjacent motif, ch 3, in next ch-7 sp work (sc, ch 3, sl st in ch-7 sp on adjacent motif, ch 3, sc)] twice. *Ch 7, work dc3tog over next 7 sts**. Ch 7, (sc, ch 7, sc) in next ch-7 sp. Rep from * to ** once more. Ch 7, sl st in sc at beg of round to join. Fasten off.

Finishing

NOTE: Edging is worked in sections. The 6 rows of pattern are worked per repeat before moving on to the next section and the 6 rows are worked back and forth in that section.

First Side

ROW 1 (SET UP SIDE EDGE): With RS facing, join with sl st to free ch-7 sp at lower edge of motif 1 (see Construction Diagram). **[Ch 3, sc] 4 times along lower edge of Motif 1, do not turn.

ROW 2: Work 9 dc in corner join before next motif, sl st in next ch-7 sp on adjoining motif.

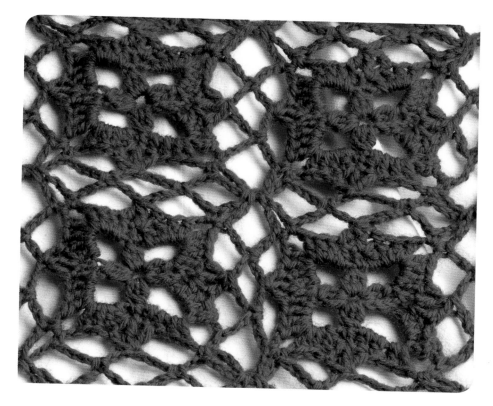

ROW 3: Ch 3, sc in same ch-7 sp on motif, turn, ch 2, sk last dc worked in prev row, dc in next st, *ch 2, sk next dc, dc in next dc; rep from * twice, ch 2, sl st in ch-3 sp along side edge of adjacent motif.

ROW 4: Ch 3, sl st in next ch-3 sp along side edge, turn, *work 4 dc in next ch-2 sp. Rep from *across, sl st in next ch-7 sp along side edge of adjacent motif.

ROW 5: Ch 3, sc in same ch-7 sp along side edge of adjacent motif, turn, ch 2, sk next dc, dc in next dc. *Ch 2, sk next dc, dc in next dc. Rep from * across, sl st in next ch-3 sp along side edge of adjacent motif.

ROW 6: Ch 3, sl st in next ch-3 sp along side edge of adjacent motif, turn, sk first ch-2 sp, *work 4 dc in next ch-2 sp. Rep from * 8 times. Sl st in next ch-7 sp on adjacent motif, work 9 dtr in same sp, sl st in same ch-7 sp.

Rep from ** for remainder of shawl's edging.

Second Side

With RS facing, join with sl st to free ch-7 sp at lower edge of motif 64. Rep first side across second side.

Wash, block to finished measurements (refer to the Construction Diagram at right), and let dry. Weave in loose ends.

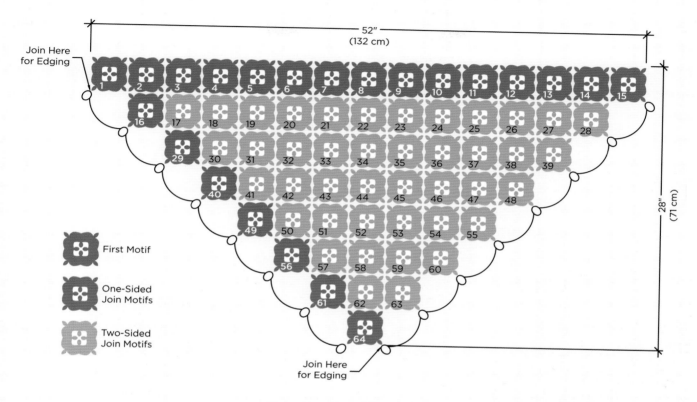

52" (132 cm)

28" (71 cm)

Join Here for Edging

Join Here for Edging

First Motif

One-Sided Join Motifs

Two-Sided Join Motifs

Construction Diagram

Kristin Omdahl writes knitting and crochet books, including *Wrapped in Crochet, Crochet So Fine, A Knitting Wrapsody,* and *Seamless Crochet* (all from Interweave). She also teaches knitting and crochet in DVD workshops, fishes with her son, and enjoys running barefoot on the beach. She writes about it all on her website, styledbykristin.com.

If you had only one ball of yarn... I would make a lacy scarf because it is something that can be worn with almost any outfit, especially if the yarn is one of your signature colors. Something that luxurious is guaranteed to feel wonderful against your neck.

linked jacket

robyn chachula

I was once asked if you could crochet a jacket out of just a few balls of yarn, and I really could not imagine that it would work. However, that's where my competitive side stepped in and I thought, "Why not?" Using chain and single crochet stitches to maximize the yarn used, I created this very cute and versatile jacket design.

MATERIALS

yarn: Worsted weight (#4 Medium).

Shown: Naturally Caron, Country (75% microdenier acrylic, 25% Merino wool; 185 yd [170 m]/3 oz [85 g]): #0017 claret, 4 (4, 5, 5, 6) balls.

hook: H/8 (5.0 mm) or hook needed to obtain gauge.

notions: Tapestry needle for weaving in ends; spray bottle with water and straight pins for blocking; 2 hook and eyes.

GAUGE

18 sts by 17 rows = 4" × 4" (10 × 10 cm) in stitch pattern.

FINISHED SIZE

S (M, L, XL, 2XL) jacket is sized to fit 32 (36, 39, 42, 46)" (81.5 [91.5, 99, 106.5, 117] m) bust circumference with a close fit. Sample shown is a size M (36" [91.5 cm] bust circumference).

finished bust: 32 (36, 40, 43, 47)" (81.5 [91.5, 101.5, 109, 119.5] cm).

finished length: 20¼ (20¼, 23, 23, 23)" (51 [51, 58, 58, 58] cm).

{notes}

* Jacket is worked in vertical rows, from side seam to side seam on back panel, then yarn is joined for each front panel and worked sideways as well.

* Sl sts are not included in st counts.

schematics

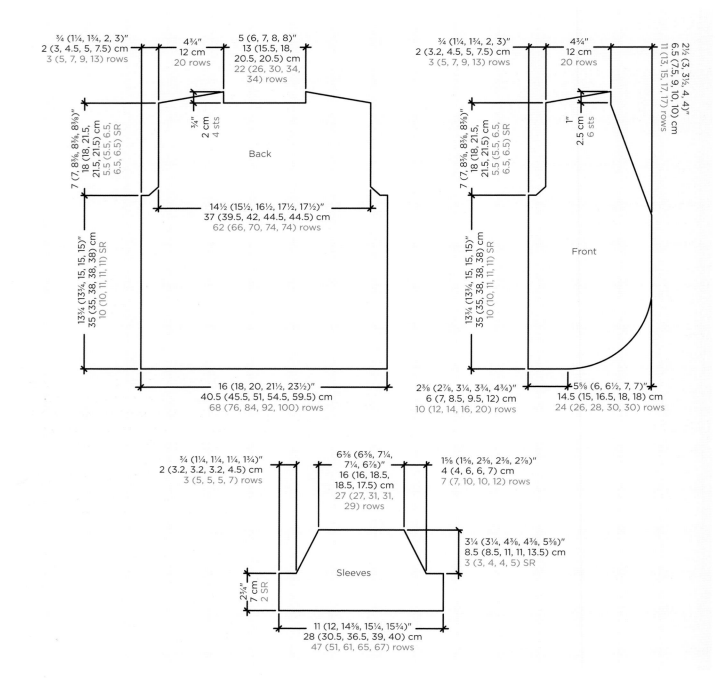

¾ (1¼, 1¾, 2, 3)"
2 (3, 4.5, 5, 7.5) cm
3 (5, 7, 9, 13) rows

4¾"
12 cm
20 rows

5 (6, 7, 8, 8)"
13 (15.5, 18, 20.5, 20.5) cm
22 (26, 30, 34, 34) rows

¾"
2 cm
4 sts

Back

7 (7, 8⅜, 8⅝, 8⅜)"
18 (18, 21.5, 21.5, 21.5) cm
5.5 (5.5, 6.5, 6.5, 6.5) SR

14½ (15½, 16½, 17½, 17½)"
37 (39.5, 42, 44.5, 44.5) cm
62 (66, 70, 74, 74) rows

13¾ (13¾, 15, 15, 15)"
35 (35, 38, 38, 38) cm
10 (10, 11, 11, 11) SR

16 (18, 20, 21½, 23½)"
40.5 (45.5, 51, 54.5, 59.5) cm
68 (76, 84, 92, 100) rows

¾ (1¼, 1¾, 2, 3)"
2 (3.2, 4.5, 5, 7.5) cm
3 (5, 7, 9, 13) rows

4¾"
12 cm
20 rows

2½ (3, 3½, 4, 4)"
6.5 (7.5, 9, 10, 10) cm
11 (13, 15, 17, 17) rows

1"
2.5 cm
6 sts

Front

7 (7, 8⅜, 8⅝, 8⅜)"
18 (18, 21.5, 21.5, 21.5) cm
5.5 (5.5, 6.5, 6.5, 6.5) SR

13¾ (13¾, 15, 15, 15)"
35 (35, 38, 38, 38) cm
10 (10, 11, 11, 11) SR

2⅜ (2⅞, 3¼, 3¾, 4¾)"
6 (7, 8.5, 9.5, 12) cm
10 (12, 14, 16, 20) rows

5⅝ (6, 6½, 7, 7)"
14.5 (15, 16.5, 18, 18) cm
24 (26, 28, 30, 30) rows

¾ (1¼, 1¼, 1¼, 1¾)"
2 (3.2, 3.2, 3.2, 4.5) cm
3 (5, 5, 5, 7) rows

6⅜ (6⅜, 7¼, 7¼, 6⅞)"
16 (16, 18.5, 18.5, 17.5) cm
27 (27, 31, 31, 29) rows

1⅝ (1⅝, 2⅜, 2⅜, 2⅞)"
4 (4, 6, 6, 7) cm
7 (7, 10, 10, 12) rows

3¼ (3¼, 4⅜, 4⅜, 5⅜)"
8.5 (8.5, 11, 11, 13.5) cm
3 (3, 4, 4, 5) SR

Sleeves

2¾"
7 cm
2 SR

11 (12, 14⅜, 15¼, 15¾)"
28 (30.5, 36.5, 39, 40) cm
47 (51, 61, 65, 67) rows

details

Special Stitches

Reverse Single Crochet (rev sc): Insert hook in prev st (the stitch to the right (instead of the left), yo and pull up a lp, yo and draw through both lps on hook. Stitch wil be twisted.

Chain Link Stitch Pattern (clsp)

See **Chain Link Stitch Pattern** diagram at right for assistance.

Ch 21.

ROW 1 (RS): Sc in 2nd ch from hook, sc in next ch, *ch 4, sk next 4 ch, sc in next 2 ch; rep from * across, turn—20 sts (3 SR).

ROW 2: Ch 1, sc in first 2 sc, *ch 4, sk ch 4-sp, sc in next 2 sc; rep from * across, turn.

Rep Row 2 for patt.

pattern

Back

Refer to **Stitch Diagram A** on page 132 for assistance.

Ch 63 (63, 69, 69, 69) with MC.

SIZE S ONLY:

Move to Armhole Shaping.

ROW 1 (RS): Sc in 2nd ch from hook, sc in next ch, *ch 4, sk next 4 chs, sc in next 2 ch; rep from * to end, turn—62 (68, 68, 68) sts (10 [11, 11, 11] SR).

Cont in Row 2 of clsp 1 (3, 5, 9) time(s).

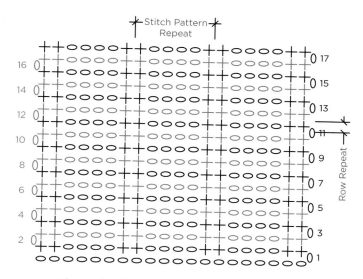

Chain Link Stitch Pattern Diagram

Armhole Shaping

S ONLY:

ROW 1: Sc in 2nd ch from hook, sc in next ch, *ch 4, sk next 4 chs, sc in next 2 ch; rep from * to last sc, 2 sc in last sc, turn—63 sts (10 SR).

M, L, XL, 2XL:

ROW 1: Ch 1, sc in next 2 sc, cont in clsp across to last sc, 2 sc in last sc, turn—63 (69, 69, 69) sts.

ALL:

ROW 2: Ch 1, 2 sc in first sc, sc in next sc, cont in clsp across to end, turn—64 (64, 70, 70, 70) sts.

ROW 3: Ch 1, sc in next 2 sc, cont in clsp across to last sc, 2 sc in last sc, turn—65 (65, 71, 71, 71) sts.

Shoulder Shaping

ROW 1: Ch 31 (31, 37, 37, 37), sc in 2nd ch from hook, sc in next 2 ch, *ch 3, sk next 3 ch, sc in next 2 sc; rep from * 3 times, cont in clsp 1 (1, 2, 2, 2) times, ch 4, sk next ch and 3 sc), sc in next 2 sc, cont in clsp across to end, turn—94 (94, 106, 106, 106) sts (16 [16, 18, 18, 18] SR).

ROW 2: Cont in clsp to ch-3 sp, *ch 3, sk ch-3 sp, sc in next 2 sc; rep from * to last sc, sc in last sc, turn.

ROW 3: Ch 1, 2 sc in first sc, sc in next 2 sc, *ch 3, sk ch-3 sp, sc in next 2 sc; rep from * to ch-4 sp, cont in clsp across to end, turn—95 (95, 107, 107, 107) sts.

ROW 4: Cont in clsp to ch-3 sp, *ch 3, sk ch-3 sp, sc in next 2 sc; rep from * to last 2 sc, sc in last 2 sc, turn.

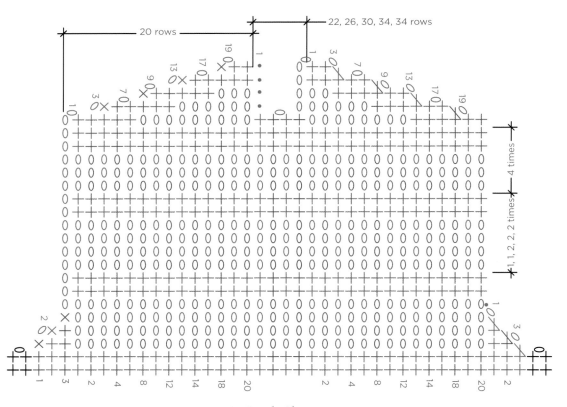

A. Back Shaping

ROW 5: Ch 1, sc in first 4 sc, *ch 3, sk ch-3 sp, sc in next 2 sc; rep from * to ch-4 sp, cont in clsp across to end, turn.

Rep Rows 4–5 once.

ROW 8: Cont in clsp to ch-3 sp, *ch 3, sk ch-3 sp, sc in next 2 sc; rep from * to last 2 sc, ch 1, sk next sc, 2 sc in last sc, turn—96 (96, 108, 108, 108) sts.

ROW 9: Ch 1, sc in first 2 sc, ch 1, sk next ch-1 sp, sc in next 2 sc, *ch 3, sk ch-3 sp, sc in next 2 sc; rep from * to ch-4 sp, cont in clsp across to end, turn.

ROW 10: Cont in clsp to ch-3 sp, *ch 3, sk ch-3 sp, sc in next 2 sc; rep from * to

last 3 sts, ch 1, sk ch-1 sp, sc in last 2 sc, turn.

Rep Rows 9–10 once.

ROW 13: Ch 1, 2 sc in first sc, ch 2, sk next sc and ch-1 sp, sc in next 2 sc, *ch 3, sk ch-3 sp, sc in next 2 sc; rep from * to ch-4 sp, cont in clsp across to end, turn—97 (97, 109, 109, 109) sts.

ROW 14: Cont in clsp to ch-3 sp, *ch 3, sk ch-3 sp, sc in next 2 sc; rep from * to last 4 sts, ch 2, sk ch-2 sp, sc in last 2 sc, turn.

ROW 15: Ch 1, sc in first 2 sc, ch 2, sk next ch-2 sp, sc in next 2 sc, *ch 3, sk

ch-3 sp, sc in next 2 sc; rep from * to ch-4 sp, cont in clsp across to end, turn.

Rep Rows 14–15 once.

ROW 18: Cont in clsp to ch-3 sp, *ch 3, sk ch-3 sp, sc in next 2 sc; rep from * to last 4 sts, ch 3, sk next ch-2 sp and sc, 2 sc in last sc, turn—98 (98, 110, 110, 110) sts (17 [17, 19, 19, 19] SR).

ROW 19: Ch 1, sc in next 2 sc, *ch 3, sk ch-3 sp, sc in next 2 sc; rep from * to ch-4 sp, cont in clsp across to end, turn.

ROW 20: Cont in clsp to ch-3 sp, *ch 3, sk ch-3 sp, sc in next 2 sc; rep from * end, turn.

Neck Shaping

ROW 1: Sl st in first 4 sts, sc in next 3 sts, *ch 3, sk next 3 ch, sc in next 2 sc; rep from * to ch-4 sp, cont in clsp across to end, turn—94 (94, 106, 106, 106) sts (16 [16, 18, 18, 18] SR).

ROW 2: Cont in clsp to ch-3 sp, *ch 3, sk ch-3 sp, sc in next 2 sc; rep from * to last sc, sc in last sc, turn.

ROW 3: Ch 1, sc in first 3 sc, *ch 3, sk ch-3 sp, sc in next 2 sc; rep from * to ch-4 sp, cont in clsp across to end, turn.

Rep Rows 2–3 nine (eleven, thirteen, fifteen, fifteen) times; rep Row 2 once.

Opposite Shoulder Shaping

ROW 1: Ch 5, sc in 2nd ch from hook, sc in next sc, ch 3, sk next 2 ch and sc, sc in next 2 sc, *ch 3, sk next 3 ch, sc in next 2 sc; rep from * to ch-4 sp, cont in clsp across to end, turn—98 (98, 110, 110, 110) sts (17 [17, 19, 19, 19] SR).

ROW 2: Cont in clsp across to ch-3 sp, *ch 3, sk ch-3 sp, sc in next 2 sc; rep from * to end, turn.

ROW 3: Ch 1, sc2tog over next 2 sc, sc in next ch, ch 2, sk ch-sp, sc in next 2 sc, *ch 3, sk ch-3 sp, sc in next 2 sc; rep from * to ch-4 sp, cont in clsp across to end, turn—97 (97, 109, 109, 109) sts.

ROW 4: Cont in clsp to ch-3 sp, *ch 3, sk ch-3 sp, sc in next 2 sc; rep from * to last 4 sts, ch 2, skip ch-2 sp, sc in last 2 sc, turn.

ROW 5: Ch 1, sc in next 2 sc, ch 2, sk ch-sp, sc in next 2 sc, *ch 3, sk ch-3 sp, sc in next 2 sc; rep from * to ch-4 sp, cont in clsp across to end, turn.

Rep Rows 4–5.

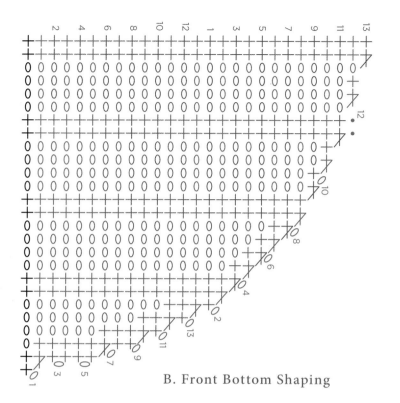

B. Front Bottom Shaping

last 2 sc, sc2tog over last 2 sc, turn—94 (94, 107, 107, 107) sts (16 [16, 18, 18, 18] SR).

ROW 19: Ch 1, sc in next 3 sc, *ch 3, sk ch-3 sp, sc in next 2 sc; rep from * to ch-4 sp, cont in clsp across to end, turn.

ROW 20: Cont in clsp to ch-3 sp, *ch 3, sk ch-3 sp, sc in next 2 sc; rep from * to last 3 sc, sc in last 3 sc, fasten off.

Opposite Armhole Shaping

ROW 1: Sk 5 (5, 6, 6, 6) ch-sps, join yarn to next ch with sl st, ch 1, sc2tog over next 2 ch, sc in next ch, sc in next 2 sc, cont in clsp across to end, turn—64 (64, 70, 70, 70) sts.

ROW 2: Cont in clsp across to last 4 sc, sc in next 2 sc, sc2tog over last 2 sc, turn—63 (63, 69, 69, 69) sts.

ROW 3: Ch 1, sc2tog over next 2 sc, sc in next sc, cont in clsp across to end, turn—62 (62, 68, 68, 68) sts (10 [10, 11, 11, 11] SR).

S ONLY:
Fasten off.

M, L, XL, 2XL:
Rep Row 2 of clsp 2 (4, 6, 10) times, do not fasten off.

Right Front

M, L, XL, 2XL ONLY:
Cont in Row 2 of clsp 2 (4, 6, 10) times.

ALL:
Rep Back Armhole Shaping and Back Shoulder Shaping through Row 7.

ROW 8: Cont in clsp to ch-3 sp, *ch 3, sk ch-3 sp, sc in next 2 sc; rep from * to last 4 sts, ch 1, sk 1 ch, sc in next ch, sc2tog over last 2 sc, turn—96 (96, 108, 108, 108) sts.

ROW 9: Ch 1, sc in next 2 sc, ch 1, sk ch-sp, sc in next 2 sc, *ch 3, sk ch-3 sp, sc in next 2 sc; rep from * to ch-4 sp, cont in clsp across to end, turn.

ROW 10: Cont in clsp to ch-3 sp, *ch 3, sk ch-3 sp, sc in next 2 sc; rep from * to last 3 sts, ch 1, sk ch sp, sc in last 2 sc, turn.

Rep Rows 9–10.

ROW 13: Ch 1, sc2tog over next 2 sc, sc in next ch-1 sp, sc in next 2 sc, *ch 3, sk ch-3 sp, sc in next 2 sc; rep from * to ch-4 sp, cont in clsp across to end, turn—95 (95, 108, 108, 108) sts.

ROW 14: Cont in clsp to ch-3 sp, *ch 3, sk ch-3 sp, sc in next 2 sc; rep from * to last 2 sc, sc in last 2 sc, turn.

ROW 15: Ch 1, sc in next 4 sc, *ch 3, sk ch-3 sp, sc in next 2 sc; rep from * to ch-4 sp, cont in clsp across to end, turn.

Rep Rows 14–15.

ROW 18: Cont in clsp to ch-3 sp, *ch 3, sk ch-3 sp, sc in next 2 sc; rep from * to

Bottom Shaping

Refer to **Stitch Diagram B** at left for assistance.

ROW 1: Ch 1, sc2tog over first 2 sc, sc in next ch, ch 3, sk ch-sp, sc in next 2 sc, cont in clsp to ch-3 sp, *ch 3, sk ch-3 sp, sc in next 2 sc; rep from * to last 2 sc, ch 1, sk next sc, 2 sc in last sc, turn—96 (96, 108, 108, 108) sts.

ROW 2: Ch 1, sc in first 2 sc, ch 1, sk next ch-1 sp, sc in next 2 sc, *ch 3, sk ch-3 sp, sc in next 2 sc; rep from * to ch-4 sp, cont in clsp across to last ch-sp, ch 3, sk ch-3 sp, sc in last 2 sc, turn.

ROW 3: Ch 1, sc in first 2 sc, ch 3, sk ch 3-sp, sc in next 2 sc, cont in clsp to ch-3 sp, *ch 3, sk ch-3 sp, sc in next 2 sc; rep from * to last 3 sts, ch 1, sk ch-1 sp, sc in last 2 sc, turn.

Rep Rows 2–3 once.

ROW 6: Ch 1, 2 sc in first sc, ch 2, sk next sc and ch-1 sp, sc in next 2 sc, *ch 3, sk ch-3 sp, sc in next 2 sc; rep from * to ch-4 sp, cont in clsp across to last 5 sts, ch 2, sk 2 ch, sc in last ch, sc2tog over last 2 sc, turn—96 (96, 108, 108, 108) sts.

ROW 7: Ch 1, sc in first 2 sc, ch 2, sk ch-sp, cont in clsp to ch-3 sp, *ch 3, sk ch-3 sp, sc in next 2 sc; rep from * to last 4 sts, ch 2, sk ch-2 sp, sc in last 2 sc, turn.

ROW 8: Ch 1, sc in next 2 sc, ch 2, sk next ch-2 sp, sc in next 2 sc, *ch 3, sk ch-3 sp, sc in next 2 sc; rep from * to ch-4 sp, cont in clsp across to last 4 sts, ch 2, sk ch 2-sp, sc in last 2 sc, turn.

ROW 9: Ch 1, sc2tog over next 2 sc, sc in next ch, ch 1, sk next ch, cont in clsp to ch-3 sp, *ch 3, sk ch-3 sp, sc in next

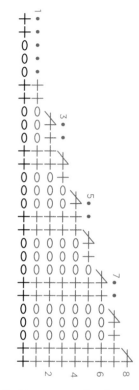

C. Front Neck Shaping

2 sc; rep from * to last 4 sts, ch 2, sk ch-2 sp, sc in last 2 sc, turn—95 (95, 107, 107, 107) sts.

ROW 10: Ch 1, sc in first 2 sc, ch 2, sk next ch-2 sp, sc in next 2 sc, *ch 3, sk ch-3 sp, sc in next 2 sc; rep from * to ch-4 sp, cont in clsp across to last 3 sts, ch 1, sk ch-1 sp, sc in last 2 sc, turn.

ROW 11: Ch 1, sc2tog over next 2 sc, sc in next ch-1 sp, sc in next 2 sc, cont in clsp to ch-3 sp, *ch 3, sk ch-3 sp, sc in next 2 sc; rep from * to last 4 sts, ch 3, sk next ch-2 sp and next sc, 2 sc in last sc, turn—95 (95, 107, 107, 107) sts.

ROW 12: Ch 1, sc in first 2 sc, *ch 3, sk ch-3 sp, sc in next 2 sc; rep from * to ch-4 sp, cont in clsp across to last 2 sc, sc in last 2 sc, turn.

ROW 13: Ch 1, sc2tog over next 2 sc, sc in next 2 sc, cont in clsp to ch-3 sp, *ch 3, sk ch-3 sp, sc in next 2 sc; rep from * end, turn—94 (94, 106, 106, 106) sts.

Neck Shaping

Refer to **Stitch Diagram C** at left for assistance.

ROW 1: Sl st in first 5 sts, sc in next 2 sc, *ch 3, sk next 3 ch, sc in next 2 sc; rep from * to ch-4 sp, cont in clsp across to last sc, sc in last sc, turn—89 (89, 101, 101, 101) sts.

ROW 2: Ch 1, sc2tog over next 2 sc, sc in next sc, cont in clsp to ch-3 sp, *ch 3, sk ch-3 sp, sc in next 2 sc; rep from * to last 3 ch, sc in next sc, sc2tog over next 2 ch, turn, leaving remaining sts unworked—85 (85, 97, 97, 97) sts.

ROW 3: Sl st in next 2 sts, sc2tog over next 2 sc, sc in next ch, ch 2, sc in next 2 sc, *ch 3, sk ch-3 sp, sc in next 2 sc; rep from * to ch-4 sp, cont in clsp across to last 6 sts, ch 3, sk 3 ch, sc in last ch, sc2tog over last 2 sc, turn—81 (81, 93, 93, 93) sts.

ROW 4: Ch 1, sc2tog over first 2 sc, sc in next ch, ch 2, sk next 2 ch, cont in clsp to ch-3 sp, *ch 3, sk ch-3 sp, sc in next 2 sc; rep from * to last 2 ch, sc2tog over last 2 ch, turn, leaving remaining sts unworked—77 (77, 89, 89, 89) sts.

ROW 5: Sl st in next 2 sts, sc2tog over next 2 sts, sc in next st, ch 1, sk next ch, sc in next 2 sc, *ch 3, sk ch-3 sp, sc in next 2 sc; rep from * to ch-4 sp, cont in clsp across to last 4 sts, ch 1, sk 1 ch, sc in last ch, sc2tog over last 2 sc, turn—73 (73, 85, 85, 85) sts.

ROW 6: Ch 1, sc2tog over next 2 sc, sc in next sts, cont in clsp to ch-3 sp, ch 3, sk ch-3 sp, sc in next sc, sc2tog over next 2 sts, turn, leaving remaining sts unworked—69 (69, 81, 81, 81) sts.

ROW 7: Sl st in first 2 sc, sc2tog over first 2 ch, sc in next ch, sc in next 2 sc, cont in clsp across to last 2 sts, sc2tog over last 2 sc, turn—65 (65, 77, 77, 77) sts.

ROW 8: Ch 1, sc2tog over next 2 sc, sc in next sc, cont in clsp to last 8 sts, ch 3, sk next 3 ch, sc in next ch, sc2tog over last 2 sc, turn, leaving remaining sts unworked—61 (61, 73, 73, 73) sts.

ROW 9: Sl st in first 2 sts, sc2tog over next 2 ch, sc in next ch, sc in next 2 sc, cont in clsp across to last 6 sts, ch 2, sk 2 ch, sc in next ch, sc2tog over next 2 sts, turn, leaving remaining st unworked—56 (56, 68, 68, 68) sts.

ROW 10: Ch 1, sk first sc, sc2tog over next 2 sts, sc in next 3 sts, cont in clsp to last 4 ch, ch 3, sk 3 ch, sc in last ch, sc2tog over next 2 sc, turn, leaving remaining sts unworked—51 (51, 63, 63, 63) sts.

ROW 11: Sl st in next 2 sc, sc2tog over next 2 ch, sc in next ch, sc in next 2 sc, cont in clsp across to last 3 sts, sc2tog over next 2 sc, turn, leaving remaining st unworked—46 (46, 58, 58, 58) sts. S only: Fasten off.

M, L, XL, 2XL ONLY:

ROW 12: Sl st in next 2 sts, sc2tog over next 2 sts, sc in next st, ch 1, sk next ch,

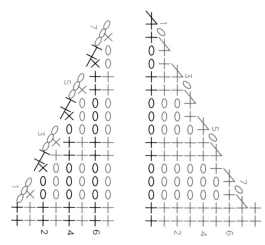

D. Cap Shaping

sc in next 2 sc, cont in clsp to last 4 ch, ch 3, sk 3 ch, sc in last ch, sc2tog over next 2 sc, turn, leaving remaining sts unworked—40 (40, 52, 52, 52) sts.

ROW 13: Sl st in next 2 sc, sc2tog over next 2 ch, sc in next ch, sc in next 2 sc, cont in clsp across to last 3 sc, sc2tog over next 2 sc, turn—34 (34, 46, 46, 46) sts. M only: Fasten off.

L, XL, 2XL ONLY:
Rep Rows 12–13 once (twice, twice) fasten off—34 (22, 22) sts.

Left Front

With WS facing, join yarn to first ch of foundation ch at base of Row 1 of Back Panel. Cont in directions for Front Panel to end, fasten off.

Sleeves (make 2)

Ch 15 (15, 15, 15, 15).

ROW 1 (RS): Sc in 2nd ch from hook, sc in next ch, *ch 4, sk next 4 chs, sc in next 2 ch; rep from * to end, turn—14 (14, 14, 14, 14) sts (2 [2, 2, 2, 2] SR).

Cont in Row 2 of clsp 2 (4, 4, 6, 6) times.

Cap Increase Shaping

Refer to **Stitch Diagram D** above for assistance.

ROW 1: Ch 3 (counts as dc), 2 sc in next sc, cont in clsp across to end, turn—16 (16, 16, 16) sts.

ROW 2: Ch 1, cont in clsp across to last sc, ch 2, (sc, dc) in top of tch, turn—18 (18, 18, 18) sts.

ROW 3: Ch 3 (counts as dc), 2 sc in first dc, ch 3, sk next sc and next ch-2 sp, sc in next 2 sc, cont in clsp across to end, turn—20 (20, 20, 20, 20) sts.

ROW 4: Ch 1, cont in clsp across to ch-3 sp, ch 3, sk next ch-sp, sc in next 2 sc, ch 1, (sc, dc) in top of tch, turn—22 (22, 22, 22, 22) sts.

ROW 5: Ch 3 (counts as dc), sc in first dc, ch 3, sk next sc and next ch-1 sp, sc in next 2 sc, ch 3, sk next ch-3 sp, sc in next 2 sc, cont in clsp across to end, turn—24 (24, 24, 24, 24) sts.

ROW 6: Ch 1, cont in clsp across to ch-3 sp, ch 3, sk next ch-sp, sc in next 2 sc, ch 3, sk next ch-3 sp, sc in next sc, (2 sc, dc) in top of tch, turn—26 (26, 26, 26) sts.

ROW 7: Ch 3 (counts as dc), sc in first dc, ch 2, sk next sc, sc in next 2 sc, *ch 3, sk next ch-sp, sc in next 2 sc; rep from * once, cont in clsp across to end, turn—28 (28, 28, 28, 28) sts.

S, M ONLY:

ROW 8: Ch 1, cont in clsp across to ch-3 sp, *ch 3, sk next ch-sp, sc in next 2 sc; rep from * twice, ch 3, sk next ch-sp, 2 sc in top of tch, turn, cont to Cap directions—29 (29) sts.

L, XL, 2XL ONLY:

ROW 8: Ch 1, cont in clsp across to ch-3 sp, *ch 3, sk ch-sp, sc in next 2 sc; rep from * once, ch 3, sk next ch-2 sp and next sc, (2 sc, dc) in top of tch, turn—30 (30, 30) sts.

ROW 9: Ch 3 (counts as dc), sc in first dc, ch 1, sc in next 2 sc, *ch 3, sk ch-sp, sc in next 2 sc; rep from * to ch-4 sp, cont in clsp across to end, turn—32 (32, 32) sts.

ROW 10: Ch 1, cont in clsp across to ch-3 sp, *ch 3, sk ch-sp, sc in next 2 sc; rep from * twice, ch 3, sk ch-sp, (sc, dc) in top of tch, turn (L, XL only; cont to Cap directions)—34 (34, 34) sts.

2XL ONLY:

ROW 11: Ch 3 (counts as dc), 2 sc in first dc, sc in next sc, *ch 3, sk ch-sp, sc in next 2 sc; rep from * to ch-4 sp, cont in clsp across to end, turn—36 sts.

ROW 12: Ch 1, cont in clsp across to ch-3 sp, *ch 3, sk ch-sp, sc in next 2 sc; rep from * 3 times, ch 2, sk next sc, (sc, dc) in top of tch, turn, cont to Cap directions—38 sts.

Cap

ROW 1: Ch 1, (S, M, L, XL) sc in next 2 sts, (2XL) 2 sc in dc, (All sizes) *ch 3, sk ch-sp, sc in next 2 sc; rep from * to ch-4 sp, cont in clsp across to end, turn—29 (29, 34, 34, 39) sts.

ROW 2: Ch 1, cont in clsp across to ch-3 sp, *ch 3, sk ch-sp, sc in next 2 sc; rep from * to end, turn.

ROW 3: Ch 1, sc in first 2 sc, *ch 3, sk ch-sp, sc in next 2 sc; rep from * to ch-4 sp, cont in clsp across to end, turn.

Rep Rows 2–3 eleven (eleven, fourteen, fourteen, twelve) times.

2XL ONLY

Rep Row 2 once.

ROW 29: Ch 1, sc2tog over next 2 sc, sc in next ch, ch 2, sk ch-sp, sc in next 2 sc, *ch 3, sk ch-sp, sc in next 2 sc; rep from * to ch-4 sp, cont in clsp across to end, turn—38 sts.

Cap Decrease Shaping

2XL:

ROW 1: Ch 1, cont in clsp across to ch-3 sp, *ch 3, sk ch-sp, sc in next 2 sc; rep from * to last ch-sp, sc in next ch, sc2tog over next ch and sc, turn, leaving remaining sts unworked—36 sts.

2XL:

ROW 2: Ch 1, sk first sc, sc2tog over next 2 sc, sc in next sc, *ch 3, sk ch-sp, sc in next 2 sc; rep from * to ch-4 sp, cont in clsp across to end, turn—34 sts.

L, XL, 2XL:

ROW 1 (1, 3): Ch 1, cont in clsp across to ch-3 sp, *ch 3, sk ch-sp, sc in next 2 sc; rep from * to last ch-sp, ch 1, sk 1 ch, sc in next ch, sc2tog over next ch and sc, turn—32 (32, 32) sts.

L, XL, 2XL:

ROW 2 (2, 4): Ch 1, sk first sc, sc2tog over next 2 sts, sc in next 2 sc, *ch 3, sk ch-sp, sc in next 2 sc; rep from * to ch-4 sp, cont in clsp across to end, turn—30 (30, 30) sts.

ALL SIZES:

ROW 1 (1, 3, 3, 5): Ch 1, cont in clsp across to ch-3 sp, *ch 3, sk ch-sp, sc in next 2 sc; rep from * to last ch-sp, ch 2, sk 2 ch, sc in next ch, sc2tog over next 2 sc, turn, leaving remaining st un-worked—28 (28, 28, 28, 28) sts.

ROW 2 (2, 4, 4, 6): Ch 1, sk first sc, sc2tog over next 2 sts, sc in next 3 sts, *ch 3, sk ch-sp, sc in next 2 sc; rep from * to ch-4 sp, cont in clsp across to end, turn—26 (26, 26, 26, 26) sts.

ROW 3 (3, 5, 5, 7): Ch 1, cont in clsp across to ch-3 sp, *ch 3, sk ch-sp, sc in next 2 sc; rep from * to last 4 sc, ch 3, sc in next sc, sc2tog over next 2 sc, turn leaving remaining st unworked—24 (24, 24, 24, 24) sts.

ROW 4 (4, 6, 6, 8): Ch 1, sk first sc, sc-2tog over next 2 sts, sc in next st, ch 1, sk next ch, sc in next 2 sc, ch 3, sk next ch, sc in next 2 sc; rep from * to ch-4 sp, cont in clsp across to end, turn—22 (22, 22, 22, 22) sts.

ROW 5 (5, 7, 7, 9): Ch 1, cont in clsp across to ch-3 sp, ch 3, sk ch-sp, sc in next 2 sc, sc2tog over next 2 sts, turn leaving remaining st unworked—20 (20, 20, 20, 20) sts.

ROW 6 (6, 8, 8, 10): Ch 1, sk first sc, sc2tog over next 2 sc, sc in next st, ch 2, sk next 2 ch, sc in next 2 sc, cont in clsp across to end, turn—18 (18, 18, 18, 18) sts.

ROW 7 (7, 9, 9, 11): Ch 1, cont in clsp across to last ch-sp, sc in next st, sc2tog over next 2 sts, turn leaving remaining st unworked—16 (16, 16, 16, 16) sts.

ROW 8 (8, 10, 10, 12): Ch 1, sk first sc, sc2tog over next 2 sc, sc in next sc, cont in clsp across to end, turn—14 (14, 14, 14, 14) sts.

Rep Row 2 of clsp 3 (5, 5, 7, 7) times, fasten off.

Finishing

Pin Back, Front, and Sleeves to schematic measurements (see Schematics on page 130). Spritz with water and allow to dry. Pin Front and Back with right sides facing. Working through double thickness of front and back, work a row of sl sts to seam shoulders. Pin sleeves to body with right sides facing, whipstitch sleeve to body.

Edging

Join yarn to edge of sleeve or body with sl st to right side. Sc around edge, sl st to first sc, do not turn. Ch 1, reverse sc in ea sc around, sl st to first sc, fasten off.

making the most of *your yarn stash*

I organize small amounts of yarn by color—remnants can be used up in small appliqué motifs on larger projects or in freeform work. Larger amounts are organized by weight, since they can either make a project on their own or work together in a larger project. If the weight is right, I can combine wool and cotton in the same project—you just need to adapt the way you launder the finished item (use the method applicable to the most delicate fiber).

* Robyn Chachula

spa shawl top

doris chan

With its graceful curves and feminine silhouette, this top creates the impression of a belted shawl, but with greater practicality and reduced bulk. Crocheted seamlessly in a simple lace stitch pattern, the top has a soft, lovely drape thanks to the silky yarn and relaxed gauge. The bodice is a rounded shawl attached to a waistband to form a deep V front and fluttery sleeves. Stop there for the short cropped version or add a gently ruffled skirt for the tunic-length version.

MATERIALS

yarn: Sportweight (#3 Light).

Shown: NaturallyCaron.com, Spa (75% microdenier acrylic, 25% rayon from bamboo; 251 yd [230 m]/3 oz [85 g]): #0007 Naturally (Version A), 3 (4, 4, 5) skeins; #0010 Stormy Blue, 4 (5, 5, 6) skeins (Version B).

hook: H/8 (5 mm) or hook needed to obtain gauge.

notions: Stitch markers; tapestry needle for weaving in ends; two ¾–⅞" (2–2.2 cm) buttons; hook-and-eye closure; sewing needle and matching thread (or untwist a length of yarn to separate the plies and use for sewing).

GAUGE

14 Fsc, sc, or hdc = 4" (10 cm).

One pattern repeat = 2½" (6.5 cm), 4 rows = 3½" (9 cm) in Shell and V Stitch Pattern.

Note: Gauge as crocheted. Fabric is stretchy. Applying waistband, blocking, and wearing will cause fabric to relax in width and length to give finished measurements.

FINISHED SIZE

S (M, L/XL, 2XL/3XL); top is shawl-like and ample through bust and arms; waistband is overlapped, buttoned and fitted; skirt of Version B is full and relaxed over hips.

Samples shown are size S.

VERSION A

finished waist: 30½ (34, 39, 43½)" (77.5 [86.5, 99, 110.5] cm).

finished length: 15 (15¾, 15¾, 16½)" (38 [40, 40, 42] cm).

VERSION B

finished waist: 30½ (34, 39, 43½)" (77.5 [86.5, 99, 110.5] cm).

finished length: 24 (24¾, 24¾, 25½)" (61 [63, 63, 65] cm).

schematics

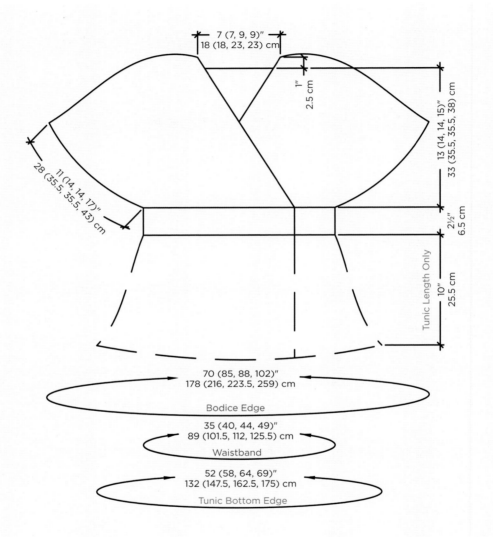

7 (7, 9, 9)"
18 (18, 23, 23) cm

1"
2.5 cm

13 (14, 14, 15)"
33 (35.5, 35.5, 38) cm

11 (14, 14, 17)"
28 (35.5, 35.5, 43) cm

2½"
6.5 cm

Tunic Length Only

10"
25.5 cm

70 (85, 88, 102)"
178 (216, 223.5, 259) cm

Bodice Edge

35 (40, 44, 49)"
89 (101.5, 112, 125.5) cm

Waistband

52 (58, 64, 69)"
132 (147.5, 162.5, 175) cm

Tunic Bottom Edge

details

Special Stitches

Foundation Single Crochet (fsc): p. 154.

Shell (sh): (3 tr, ch 1, 3 tr) in st or sp indicated.

V Stitch (v-st): (Tr, ch 1, tr) in st or sp indicated.

Increase V Stitch (inc-v): (V-st, ch 1, v-st) in st or sp indicated.

Beginning Half Double Crochet (beg-hdc): For a neater edge in hdc, use this technique to create an actual stitch at the beginning of a row. Ch 2, insert hook in 2nd ch from hook, yo and draw up a lp (2 lps on hook), insert hook in first st of row, yo and draw up a lp (3 lps on hook), yo and draw through all 3 lps on hook.

7 Treble Crochet Fan (fan): [Tr, (ch 1, tr)] 6 times in sp indicated.

Spa Shell Stitch Pattern (sssp)

Refer to **Spa Shell Stitch Pattern** diagram above right for assistance.

Foundation Row: 17 fsc, turn.

ROW 1: Ch 4, tr in first sc (counts as half v-st), sk 3 sc, sh in next sc, *sk 3 sc, v-st in next sc, sk 3 sc, sh in next sc, rep from * across to last 4 sc, end with 2 tr in last ch, turn.

ROW 2 (PATT A): Ch 4 (counts as tr), 2 tr in first tr (counts as half-shell), v-st in ch-1 sp of next sh, *sh in ch-1 sp of next v-st, v-st in ch-1 sp of next sh, rep from

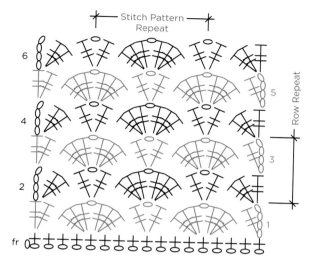

Spa Shell Stitch Pattern Diagram

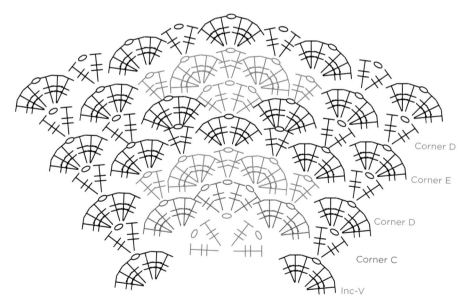

Corner Increasing

* across, end with 3 tr for half-shell in 4th ch of tch, turn.

ROW 3 (PATT B): Ch 4, tr in first tr (counts as half v-st), sh in ch-1 sp of next v-st, *v-st in ch-1 sp of next sh, sh in ch-1 sp of next v-st, rep from * across, end with 2 tr for half v-st in 4th ch of tch, turn.

Rep Rows 2–3 to desired length.

To increase in pattern at six points in the middle of the shawl, use the following insertions (referring to the **Corner Increasing** diagram on page 143 for assistance):

CORNER C: Working in sssp, in ea inc-v work [sh in first ch-1 sp, inc-v in 2nd (marked center) ch-1 sp, sh in 3rd ch-1 sp].

CORNER D: Working in sssp, in ea inc-v work (sh in first ch-1 sp, v-st in 2nd (marked center) ch-1 sp, sh in 3rd ch-1 sp).

CORNER E: Working in sssp, in marked ch-1 sp of sh at center of ea increase point, omit v-st, instead inc-v in center ch-1 sp.

To increase at the ends of rows to shape front neck edges, use the following insertions (referring to the **Front Edge Increasing** diagram above for assistance):

FRONT F: Beg with ch 5 (counts as tr, ch 1), sk first tr, 3 tr in first ch-1 sp for partial shell; work row as directed; end with 3 tr in tch-sp, ch 1, tr in 4th ch of tch for partial shell, turn.

FRONT G: Beg with ch 5, sk first tr, v-st in ch-1 sp of partial shell; work row as

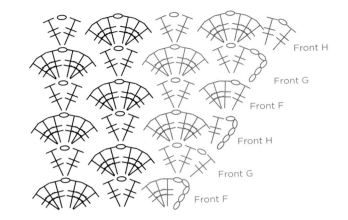

Front H
Front G
Front F
Front H
Front G
Front F

Front Edge Increasing

directed; end with v-st in tch-sp, ch 1, tr in 4th ch of tch, turn.

FRONT H: Beg with ch 5, sk first tr, tr in first ch-1 sp for beg v-st; work row as directed; end with tr in tch-sp, ch 1, tr in 4th ch of tch, turn.

pattern
(version a: cropped length)

Shawl Top is crocheted from the top down, seamlessly, beginning at back neck. The first row sets up six increase points; mark the 2nd (center) ch-1 sp of the inc-v at ea point, move markers up into the ch-1 sp at the center of ea point as you go. Shape bodice increases using insertions at Corner C, Corner D, and Corner E as directed; at the same time, shape front edges with insertions at Front F, Front G, and Front H as directed. Instructions for insertions are on page at left and above.

Bodice

Fsc 49 (49, 57, 57), turn foundation over so sc edge is on top, begin working across sc edge.

ROW 1: Ch 5 (counts as tr, ch 1), (tr, ch 1, v-st) in first sc for first inc point, sk next 3 sc, sh in next sc, sk next 3 sc, inc-v in next sc for 2nd inc point, sk next 3 sc, sh in next sc, sk next 3 sc, inc-v in next sc for 3rd inc point, sk next 3 sc, sh in next sc, sk next 3 sc, [v-st in next sc, sk next 3 sc, sh in next sc, sk next 3 sc] 1 (1, 2, 2) times, inc-v in next sc for 4th inc point, sk next 3 sc, sh in next sc, sk next 3 sc, inc-v in next sc for 5th inc point, sk next 3 sc, sh in next sc, sk next 3 sc, inc-v in last sc for 6th inc point, turn—6 (6, 7, 7) sh, inc-vs at 6 points.

SIZE S ONLY:

ROW 2: Ch 5, across first inc-v work (3 tr in first ch-1 sp, v-st in 2nd [center] ch-1 sp, sh in 3rd ch-1 sp), *v-st in ch-1 sp of next sh, across next inc-v work Corner D, v-st in ch-1 sp of next sh,

across next inc-v work Corner D*, v-st in ch-1 sp of next shell, sh in ch-1 sp of next v-st; repeat from * to * once, v-st in ch-1 sp of next sh, across last inc-v work sh in next ch-1 sp, v-st in center ch-1 sp, 3 tr in tch-sp, ch 1, tr in 4th ch of tch, turn—11 sh, plus partial sh at ea end.

ROW 3: Beg as Front G, sh in ch-1 sp of next v-st, [v-st in ch-1 sp of next sh, sh in ch-1 sp of next v-st] 11 times, end as Front G—12 sh, with a sh at ea inc point.

ROW 4: Beg as Front H, sh in ch-1 sp of next v-st, work across in sssp with

Corner E, end with sh in ch-1 sp of last v-st, end as Front H—13 sh, with inc-vs at 6 points.

ROW 5: Beg as Front F, work across in sssp with Corner D, end as Front F—18 sh, plus partial sh at ends.

ROW 6: Beg as Front G, work in sssp even across points, end as Front G—19 sh.

ROW 7: Rep Row 4—20 sh.

ROW 8: Rep Row 5—25 sh, plus partial sh at ends.

ROW 9: Rep Row 6—26 sh.

Cont to shape front neck, work even across points, cont to move m at points.

ROW 10: Beg as Front H, work sssp even, end as Front H—27 sh.

ROW 11: Beg as Front F, work sssp even, end as Front F—26 sh plus partial sh at ends.

ROW 12: Beg as Front G, work sssp even, end as Front G—27 sh.

ROW 13: Ch 4 (counts as tr), sh in ch-1 sp of next v-st, work in sssp even across, end with sh in ch-1 sp of last v-st, tr in 4th ch of tch, turn—28 sh, with sh at ea of 6 points.

SIZES M (L/XL, 2XL/3XL):

ROW 2: Ch 5, across first inc-v work (3 tr in first ch-1 sp, inc-v in 2nd (center) ch-1 sp, sh in 3rd ch-1 sp), *v-st in ch-1 sp of next sh, across next inc-v work Corner C, v-st in ch-1 sp of next sh, across next inc-v work Corner C*, [v-st in ch-1 sp of next sh, sh in ch-1 sp of next v-st] 1 (2, 2) times; rep from * to * once, v-st in ch-1 sp of next sh, across last inc-v work sh in next ch-1 sp, inc-v in center ch-1 sp, 3 tr in tch-sp, ch 1, tr in 4th ch of tch, turn—11 (12, 12) sh, plus partial sh at ea end; inc-vs at 6 points.

SIZES M (L/XL) ONLY:

ROW 3: Beg as Front G, across first inc-v work Corner D, [work in sssp to next inc-v, work Corner D] 5 times, end as Front G—18 (19) sh.

ROW 4: Beg as Front H, work in sssp even across points—19 (20) sh.

ROW 5: Beg as Front F, work in sssp with Corner E, end as Front F—18 (19) sh with partial sh at ends.

ROW 6: Beg as Front G, work in sssp with Corner D, end as Front G—25 (26) sh.

ROW 7: Rep Row 4—26 (27) sh.

ROW 8: Rep Row 5—25 (26) sh with partial sh at ends.

ROW 9: Rep Row 6—32 (33) sh.

Cont to shape front neck, work even across points, cont to move m at points.

ROW 10: Rep Row 4—33 (34) sh.

ROW 11: Beg as Front F, work sssp even, end as Front F—32 (33) sh plus partial sh at ends.

ROW 12: Beg as Front G, work in sssp even, end as Front G—33 (34) sh.

ROW 13: Rep Row 4—34 (35) sh.

ROW 14: Ch 4 (counts as tr), 2 tr in first ch-1 sp for half-sh, v-st in ch-1 sp of next sh, work in sssp even, end with v-st in ch-1 sp of last sh, 2 tr in tch-sp, tr in 4th ch of tch, turn—33 (34) sh plus half-sh at ends, with sh at ea of 6 points.

SIZE 2XL/3XL ONLY:

ROW 3: Beg as Front G, across first inc-v work Corner C, [work in sssp to next inc-v, work Corner C] 5 times, end as Front G—19 sh.

ROW 4: Beg as Front H, work in sssp with Corner D, end as Front H—26 sh.

ROW 5: Beg as Front F, work in sssp even across points, end as Front F—25 sh plus partial sh at ends.

ROW 6: Beg as Front G, work in sssp with Corner E, end as Front G—26 sh.

ROW 7: Rep Row 4—33 sh.

ROW 8: Rep Row 5—32 sh plus partial sh at ends.

ROW 9: Rep Row 6—33 sh.

ROW 10: Rep Row 4—40 sh.

Cont to shape front neck, work even across points, cont to move m at points.

ROW 11: Rep Row 5—39 sh plus partial sh at ends.

ROW 12: Beg as Front G, work sssp even, end as Front G—40 sh.

ROW 13: Beg as Front H, work sssp even, end as Front H—41 sh.

ROW 14: Same as L/XL Row 14—40 sh plus half-sh at ends.

ROW 15: Work Patt B—41 shells.

Waistband

Connect fronts and back while working a row of sc, adjusting stitch count as you work across. First row of band becomes RS of work as follows:

SIZE S ONLY:

ROW 1 (RS): Ch 1, sc in first tr, sc in ea tr and ch-1 sp to next m at ch-1 sp of sh (first point), sc in marked ch-1 sp (35 sc), sk next 7 shells (skipping 2nd m) for armhole, sc in marked ch-1 sp of next sh (3rd point), sc in ea tr and ch-1 sp to next m at ch-1 sp of sh (4th point), sc in marked ch-1 sp (51 sc), sk next 7 shells (skipping 5th m) for armhole, sc in marked ch-1 sp of next sh (6th point), sc in ea tr and ch-1 sp across, end with sc in 4th ch of tch (35 sc), turn—121 sc.

SIZE M ONLY:

ROW 1 (RS): Ch 1, sc in first tr, sc in ea tr and ch-1 sp to next m at ch-1 sp of sh (first point), sc in marked ch-1 sp (40 sc), sk next 9 sh (skipping 2nd m) for armhole, sc in marked ch-1 sp of next sh (3rd point), sc in ea of next 2 tr, sk next tr of shell, sc in next tr of v-st, sc in next ch-1 sp of v-st, sc in next tr of v-st, sk next tr of sh, sc in ea tr and ch-1 sp to sh before next m, sc in ea of next 3 tr of sh, sc in ch-1 sp, sc in ea of next 2 tr, sk next tr of sh, sc in next tr of v-st, sc in next ch-1 sp of v-st, sc in next tr of v-st, sk next tr of sh, sc in ea of next 2 tr, sc in marked ch-1 sp of sh (4th point; 57 sc), sk next 9 sh (skipping 5th m) for

armhole, sc in marked ch-1 sp of next sh (6th point), sc in ea tr and ch-1 sp across, end with sc in 4th ch of tch (40 sc), turn—137 sc.

SIZE L/XL ONLY:

ROW 1 (RS): Ch 1, sc in first tr, sc in ea tr and ch-1 sp to next m at ch-1 sp of sh (first point), sc in marked ch-1 sp (40 sc), sk next 9 sh (skipping 2nd m) for armhole, 2 sc in marked ch-1 sp of next sh (3rd point), sc in ea tr and ch-1 sp to next m at ch-1 sp of sh (4th point), 2 sc in marked ch-1 sp (63 sc), sk next 9 sh (skipping 5th m) for armhole, sc in marked ch-1 sp of next sh (6th point), sc in ea tr and ch-1 sp across, end with sc in 4th ch of tch (40 sc), turn—153 sc.

SIZE 2XL/3XL ONLY:

ROW 1 (RS): Ch 1, sc in first tr, sc in ea tr and ch-1 sp to next m at ch-1 sp of sh (first point), sc in marked ch-1 sp (45 sc), sk next 11 sh (skipping 2nd m) for armhole, sc in marked ch-1 sp of next sh (3rd point), sc in ea of next 2 tr, sk next tr of sh, sc in ea tr and ch-1 sp to next marked sh at point, sk first tr of sh, sc in ea of next 2 tr, sc in marked ch-1 sp of sh (4th point) (79 sc), sk next 11 sh (skipping 5th m) for armhole, sc in marked ch-1 sp of next sh (6th point), sc in ea tr and ch-1 sp across, end with sc in 4th ch of tch (45 sc), turn—169 sc.

ALL SIZES:

ROW 2 (WS): Beg-hdc in first sc, sk next sc, [2 hdc in next sc, sk next sc] 59 (67, 75, 83) times, hdc in last sc, turn—59 (67, 75, 83) hdc Vs plus edge sts.

ROW 3: Beg-hdc in first hdc, sk next hdc, 2 hdc in next sp bet 2 hdc (middle

of v-st), [sk next 2 hdc, 2 hdc in next sp between 2 hdc] 58 (66, 74, 82) times, sk next hdc, hdc in last hdc, turn.

ROWS 4–10: Rep Row 3 seven times.

Finishing

Front and Neck Edging

NOTE: When working sc edging across row edges, for a neater appearance and to avoid excessive gapping, insert hook under 2 strands of edge each time (rather than under the whole edge stitch). It is not critical which 2 strands; try to do it the same way each time.

Finish entire front and neck edge with sc, creating 2 buttonholes along right-hand edge of waistband as follows:

Turn, RS now facing, join yarn with sl st in first hdc row edge at lower right-hand corner of front waist.

ROW 1 (RS): Ch 1, across next 10 row edges of waistband, working under 2 strands of row edge ea time, sc in first hdc row edge, sc in next hdc row edge, ch 2, sk next 2 hdc row edges for buttonhole, sc in ea of next 3 hdc row edges, ch 2, sk next 2 hdc row edges for buttonhole, sc in next sc row edge. To allow for some give across the front neck shaping, make 7 sc across every 2 tr row edges by working: [sc in ea of 4 ch of next tr row edge, 3 sc evenly spaced along next tr row edge] 6 (7, 7, 7) times. Sizes S and 2XL only, sc in ea of next 4 ch of last tr row edge. All sizes, sc in ea ch of neck foundation. Sizes S and 2XL only, 3 sc evenly spaced along next tr row edge. All sizes [sc in ea of 4 ch of next tr row edge,

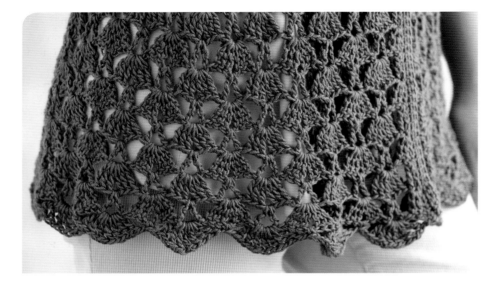

3 sc evenly spaced along next tr row edge] 6 (7, 7, 7) times, sc in next sc row edge of waistband, sc in ea of next 9 hdc row edges, turn.

ROW 2: Ch 1, sc in ea sc across, working 2 sc in ea ch-2 buttonhole sp, turn.

ROW 3: Ch 1, sc in ea sc across, fasten off.

Armhole Edging

RS of one armhole facing, join yarn with sl st in sc row edge of waistband at underarm (bet front and back sections).

FAN EDGING (RS): Ch 1, sc in same sc row edge, ch 1, [fan in ch-1 sp of next v-st of armhole, ch 1, sc in ch-1 sp of next sh of armhole, ch 1] 7 (9, 9, 11) times, fan in ch-1 sp of last v-st of armhole, ch 1, sl st in beg sc, fasten off and end yarn—8 (10, 10, 12) fans.

Make Armhole Edging around other armhole in the same way.

Weave in ends, block the top to the finished measurements (see Schematics on page 142) before attaching closures.

Closures

Try on the top after blocking and decide how much you want to overlap the front waistband ends, mark the location for 2 buttons on the outside of the left-hand front, centered under the 2 buttonholes. Mark the location for a hook-and-eye closure to secure the left-hand end of the waistband to the inside. Sew on the hook-and-eye closures.

pattern
(version b: tunic length)

Follow directions for Version A (beginning on page 144) through Waistband, but do not fasten off.

Skirt

Turn, RS now facing, work 15 (17, 19, 21) sssp repeats across waistband, working in spaces between hdc Vs ea time, with 4 inc evenly spaced for hip shaping as follows:

ROW 1 (RS): Ch 4, tr in first hdc, sk next 3 hdc, sh in next sp bet hdc (middle of hdc v-st), [sk next 4 hdc, v-st in next sp bet hdc, sk next 4 hdc, sh in next sp bet hdc] 2 (2, 2, 3) times, sk next 4 hdc, inc-v in next sp between hdc for first increase, sk next 4 hdc, sh in next sp between hdc, repeat bet [ ] 2 (3, 3, 3) times, sk next 4 hdc, inc-v in next sp bet hdc for 2nd inc, sk next 4 hdc, sh in next sp bet hdc, rep bet [ ] 2 (2, 4, 4) times, sk next 4 hdc, inc-v in next sp bet hdc for 3rd inc, sk next 4 hdc, sh in next sp between hdc, repeat between [ ] 2 (3, 3, 3) times, sk next 4 hdc, inc-v in next sp bet hdc for 4th inc, sk next 4 hdc, sh in next sp bet hdc, rep bet [ ] 2 (2, 2, 3) times, sk next 3 hdc, 2 tr in last hdc, turn—15 (17, 19, 21) sh, with 4 inc points.

ROW 2: Beg as for sssp Patt A, [work in sssp across to next inc-v, work Corner D across inc-v] 4 times, work in stitch pattern, end as sssp Patt A—18 (20, 22, 24) shells plus half-shells at ends.

ROW 3: Work sssp Patt B—19 (21, 23, 25) sh.

ROWS 4-10: Work [sssp Patt A, sssp Patt B] 3 times, then work sssp Patt A once more, turn and cont with Finishing.

Finishing

Edging

RS now facing, make Fan Edging along lower edge, then cont to finish front and neck edges as follows:

ROW 1 (RS): Ch 1, sc in first tr, ch 1, fan in ch-1 sp of next v-st, ch 1, [sc in ch-1 sp of next sh, ch 1, fan in ch-1 sp of next v-st, ch 1] across, end with sc in 4th ch of tch, rotate and work across row edges of skirt, ch 1, sc in first sc row edge, 3 sc across ea of next 10 tr row edges. In same way as Version A Front and Neck Edging Row 1, sc across waistband, making 2 buttonholes and cont around bodice. After working across 10 row edges of other side of waistband, 3 sc across ea of next 10 tr row edges of Skirt, sc in last sc row edge, turn.

ROWS 2–3: Same as Version A Front and Neck Edging Rows 2–3.

Doris Chan has produced three well-received crochet books: *Amazing Crochet Lace, Everyday Crochet,* and *Crochet Lace Innovations* (Potter Craft), as well as technical articles and hundreds of designs for magazines, books, and yarn company catalogs. Her latest venture is DJC Designs, a line of self-published patterns available exclusively at designingvashti.com. Doris is an active professional member of CGOA and is a CYCA-certified crochet instructor. Visit Doris at her blog, dorischancrochet.com.

If you had only one ball of yarn… For me, exploded lace is the way to go with just about any yarn. My current obsession is Broomstick Lace, an awesome technique for special yarns.

SYMBOL CROCHET BASICS

The key to understanding **crochet symbols** is that each symbol represents a crochet stitch. I like to think of them as little stick diagrams of the actual stitch. Let's look at the smallest stitch, the chain. The symbol is an oval. Why an oval? Well, think about making a chain stitch: it's a simple loop pulled through another loop. That loop looks a lot like an oval, doesn't it? The international crochet symbols try to mimic the actual stitch as much as they can in the little stick diagram.

Next is the slip stitch, which is a filled dot. It is tiny—almost invisible—just like the actual stitch. The single crochet is a squat cross, again just like the stitch. The half double crochet is slightly taller than the single crochet. The double crochet is taller than the half double and has an extra cross in its middle. From the double crochet up, the little cross tells you how many yarnovers you have before you insert your hook. Go ahead, make a double crochet. Now look at your stitch: do you see the little cross in the middle of the stitch? That is why the double crochet symbol has that bar in the middle of its post. The rest of the symbols fall in line with the same reasoning. If the stitch is short, the symbol will be short; if the stitch puffs out, the symbol will as well.

To read **granny square diagrams,** you need to start in the center just like you would to crochet. Following the symbol key, crochet the stitches you see. The numbers on the diagram let you know where the beginning of each round is so you can keep track of where you are. Granny square diagrams feature each round in a new color so it's easy to keep track of which round you are on.

Stitch pattern diagrams are not much different than granny square diagrams. The key difference is that instead of crocheting in the round, you crochet back and forth in turned rows. Therefore, when you are reading the diagram, you need to start at the bottom foundation chain. Crochet as many chains as the diagram shows. Then, following the symbol key, crochet the stitches you see for the first row. At the end of the row, turn, and continue crocheting the stitches you see for the following rows. The numbers on the diagram let you know where the beginning of each row is so you can keep track of where you are. Each diagram has a new color for each row so it's easy to keep track of which row you are on.

Top Six Rules of Symbol Crochet

Remembering these simple rules will help you as you follow the symbol crochet diagrams featured throughout the book. These rules are a summary of the crochet symbol basics we just reviewed.

1. Each symbol represents one stitch to crochet. (See chart at right for a list of symbols and their stitches.)

2. Each symbol is a tiny stick diagram of the actual stitch. So the taller or fatter the symbol, the taller or fatter the stitch it represents.

3. Each row or round is a different color in the diagrams to help you keep track of which one you are working on.

4. Each row or round has a numeral next to the beginning turning chain, indicating the start of the row or round and the row or round number.

5. Granny square diagrams start in the center and increase outward, just as you would crochet them.

6. Stitch pattern diagrams work rows back and forth and indicate in brackets how many stitches (SR) or rows (RR) to repeat in a design.

crochet symbols

- ⬮ ch
- • sl st
- + sc
- sc2tog
- esc
- fsc
- sc in middle bar
- sc spike
- BPsc
- hdc
- hdc2tog
- 3hdc-cl
- dc
- fdc
- crochet spike

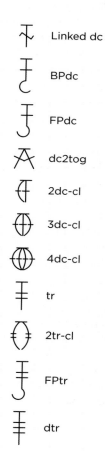

- Linked dc
- BPdc
- FPdc
- dc2tog
- 2dc-cl
- 3dc-cl
- 4dc-cl
- tr
- 2tr-cl
- FPtr
- dtr

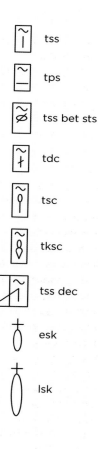

- tss
- tps
- tss bet sts
- tdc
- tsc
- tksc
- tss dec
- esk
- lsk

GLOSSARY

abbreviations

bpdc	back post double crochet
beg	begin/beginning
bet	between
blp	through back loop(s) only
BP	back post
CC	contrasting color
ch	chain
ch-sp	chain space
cm	centimeter(s)
cont	continue
dc	double crochet
dc-cl	double crochet cluster
dec	decrease/decreases/decreasing
dtr	double treble crochet
ea	each
edc	extended double crochet
esc	extended single crochet
esk	edge solomon's knot
est	established
fdc	foundation double crochet
flp	through front loop(s) only
foll	follow/follows/following
FP	front post

fr	foundation row
fsc	foundation single crochet
fwd	forward pass
g	gram(s)
hdc	half double crochet
hdc-cl	half double crochet cluster
inc	increase/increases/increasing
lp(s)	loop(s)
lsk	long solomon's knot
MC	main color
m	marker
mo(s)	month(s)
opp	opposite
patt	pattern
pm	place marker
prev	previous
rem	remain/remaining
rep	repeat(s)
rnd	round
RS	right side
RetP	return pass
sc	single crochet
sh	shell

sk	skip
sl st	slip stitch
SP	stitch pattern
st(s)	stitch(es)
tch	turning chain
tog	together
tr	treble crochet
tr-cl	treble crochet cluster
tss	Tunisian simple stitch
tps	Tunisian purl stitch
tdc	Tunisian double crochet
tsc	Tunisian singe crochet
tksc	Tunisian knitwise single crochet
WS	wrong side
yd	yard(s)
yo	yarn over
*	repeat instructions following asterisk as directed
**	repeat all instructions between asterisks as directed
( )	alternate instructions and/or measurements
[ ]	work bracketed instructions specified number of times

terms and techniques

Gauge

The quickest way to check gauge is to make a square of fabric about 4″ wide by 4″ tall (10 × 10 cm; or motif indicated in pattern for gauge) with the suggested hook size and in the indicated stitch. If your measurements match the measurements of the pattern's gauge, congratulations! If you have too many stitches, try going up a hook size. If you have too few stitches, try going down a hook size. Crochet another swatch with the new hook until your gauge matches what is indicated in the pattern.

If the gauge has been measured after blocking, be sure to wet your swatch and block it before taking measurements to check gauge. Wet-blocking drastically effects the gauge measurement, especially in lace stitch work.

Blocking

Blocking allows the fabric to relax and ensures proper shape, measurements, and drape of the fabric. After time and wear, you will still want to block your garment after washings to bring it back to its original shape. Remember to treat wool fibers carefully when wetting or washing to block. Avoid felting by staying away from hot water and agitation (from a washing machine or water removal by hand). Also remember to keep synthetic fibers (e.g., acrylic) away from high heat.

Blocking can be achieved by spray-blocking, wet-blocking, or steam-blocking. In spray-blocking, you pin your project to its schematic size and spray lightly with water. Wet-blocking involves pinning a wet piece to finished measurements and allowing the piece to air-dry. Steam-blocking is achieved by pinning the piece to finished measurements (dry), using a steamer or steam iron to gently steam the entire piece (do not touch the iron directly to the fabric), and then allowing the piece to air-dry.

Row Repeat (RR)

The indicated row or rows that are repeated to create a crochet fabric.

Stitch Pattern Repeat (SR)

The indicated stitches that are duplicated on the same row to create the stitch pattern.

crochet stitches

Crochet Chain (ch)

Make a slipknot and place it on crochet hook. *Yarn over hook and draw through loop on hook. Repeat from * for the desired number of stitches.

Slip Stitch (sl st)

*Insert hook into stitch, yarn over hook and draw loop through stitch and loop on hook, repeat from *.

Single Crochet (sc)

Insert hook into a stitch, yarn over hook and draw up a loop (figure 1), yarn over hook and draw it through both loops on hook (figure 2).

figure 1

figure 2

Extended Single Crochet (esc)

Insert hook into next stitch, yarn over hook and draw up a loop, yarn over hook, draw through 1 loop on hook, yarn over hook, draw through remaining 2 loops on hook.

Foundation Single Crochet (fsc)

Ch 2, insert hook in 2nd ch from hook, pull up loop, yarn over hook, draw through 1 loop (the "ch"), yarn over hook, draw through 2 loops (the "sc"), *insert hook under 2 loops of the "ch" stitch of last stitch and pull up loop, yarn over hook and draw through 1 loop, yarn over and draw through 2 loops, repeat from * for length of foundation.

Single Crochet 2 Together (sc2tog)

Insert hook into indicated stitch or space, yarn over hook and draw up a loop, insert hook into next stitch, yarn over hook and draw up a loop, yarn over hook, draw through all 3 loops on hook—1 decrease made.

Single Crochet 3 Together (sc3tog)

Insert hook into indicated stitch or sace, yarn over hook, pull up a loop, [insert hook into next st, yarn over hook and draw up a loop] twice, yarn over hook, draw through all 4 loops on hook—2 decreases made.

Single Crochet 4 Together (sc4tog)

Insert hook into indicated stitch or space, yarn over hook, pull up a loop, [insert hook into next stitch, yarn over hook and draw up a loop] 3 times, yarn over hook, draw through all 5 loops on hook—3 decreases made.

Adjustable Ring

Make a large loop with the yarn (figure 1). Holding the loop with your fingers, insert hook into loop and pull working yarn through loop (figure 2). Yarn over hook, pull through loop on hook.

Continue to work indicated number of stitches into loop (figure 3; shown in single crochet). Pull on yarn tail to close loop (figure 4).

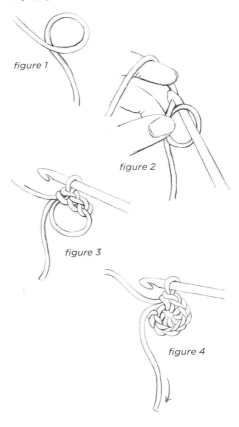

figure 1

figure 2

figure 3

figure 4

Half Double Crochet (hdc)

*Yarn over hook, insert hook into next stitch, yarn over hook and draw up a loop (3 loops on hook), yarn over hook (figure 1) and draw it through all loops on hook (figure 2), repeat from *.

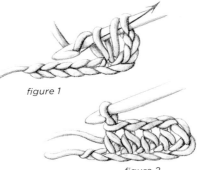

figure 1

figure 2

2 Half Double Crochet Cluster (2hdc-cl)

[Yarn over hook, insert hook into indicated stitch or space, yarn over hook, draw up loop] twice, yarn over hook, draw through all 5 loops on hook.

3 Half Double Crochet Cluster (3hdc-cl)

[Yarn over hook, insert hook into indicated stitch or space, yarn over hook, draw up loop] 3 times, yarn over hook, draw through all 7 loops on hook.

Double Crochet (dc)

*Yarn over hook, insert hook into next stitch, yarn over hook and draw up a loop (3 loops on hook; **figure 1**), yarn over hook and draw it through 2 loops (**figure 2**), yarn over hook and draw it through remaining 2 loops on hook (**figure 3**), repeat from *.

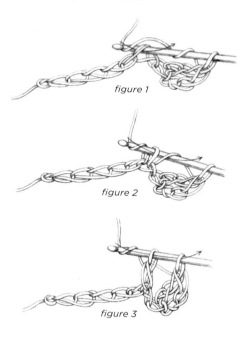

figure 1

figure 2

figure 3

Double Crochet 2 Together (dc2tog)

[Yarn over hook, insert hook into next indicated stitch or space, yarn over hook and draw up a loop, yarn over hook and draw yarn through 2 loops on hook] twice, yarn over hook and draw yarn through remaining 3 loops on hook—1 decrease made.

Double Crochet 3 Together (dc3tog)

[Yarn over hook, insert hook into next indicated stitch or space, yarn over hook and draw up a loop, yarn over hook and draw yarn through 2 loops] 3 times, yarn over hook and draw yarn through remaining 4 loops on hook—2 decreases made.

2 Double Crochet Cluster (2dc-cl)

[Yarn over hook, insert hook into indicated stitch or space, yarn over hook, draw up loop, yarn over hook, draw through 2 loops on hook] twice in same stitch, yarn over hook, draw through remaining 3 loops on hook.

3 Double Crochet Cluster (3dc-cl)

[Yarn over hook, insert hook into indicated stitch, yarn over hook, draw up loop, yarn over hook, draw through 2 loops on hook] 3 times in same stitch, yarn over hook, draw through remaining 4 loops on hook.

4 Double Crochet Cluster (4dc-cl)

[Yarn over hook, insert hook into indicated stitch or space, yarn over hook, draw up loop, yarn over hook, draw through 2 loops on hook] 4 times, yarn over hook, draw through remaining 5 loops on hook.

Front Post double crochet (FPdc)

Yarn over hook, insert hook from front to back to front around the post of indicated stitch, yarn over hook, pull up a loop, yarn over hook, draw through 2 loops on hook, yarn over hook, draw through last 2 loops on hook.

Back Post double crochet (BPdc)

Yarn over hook, insert hook from back to front to back around the post of indicated stitch, yarn over hook, pull up a loop, yarn over hook, draw through 2 loops on hook, yarn over hook, draw through last 2 loops on hook.

Treble Crochet (tr)

*Yarn over hook twice, insert hook into next indicated stitch, yarn over hook and draw up a loop (4 loops on hook; **figure 1**), yarn over hook and draw it through 2 loops (**figure 2**), yarn over hook and draw it through the next 2 loops, yarn over hook and draw it through remaining 2 loops on hook (**figure 3**), repeat from *.

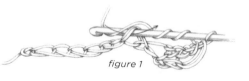

figure 1

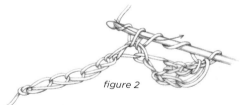

figure 2

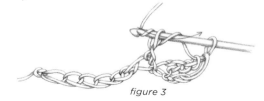

figure 3

2 Treble Crochet Cluster (2tr-cl)

*Yarn over hook twice, insert hook into indicated stitch or space, yarn over hook, draw up loop, [yarn over hook, draw through 2 loops on hook] twice, repeat from * once, yarn over hook, draw through remaining 3 loops on hook.

3 Treble Crochet Cluster (3tr-cl)

*Yarn over hook twice, insert hook into indicated stitch or space, yarn over hook, draw up loop, [yarn over hook, draw through 2 loops on hook] twice, rep from * twice, yarn over hook, draw through remaining 4 loops on hook.

Double Treble Crochet (dtr)

*Yarn over hook 3 times, insert hook into indicated stitch or space, yarn over hook, draw up a loop (5 loops on hook), [yarn over hook and draw it through 2 loops on hook] 4 times.

tunisian crochet stitches

Tunisian Simple Stitch (tss)

ROW 1 (RS) FWD: Pull up loop in 2nd ch from hook and each ch across. **RetP:** Yarn over hook, pull through 1 loop on hook, *yarn over hook, pull through 2 loops on hook, repeat from * to end.

ROW 2 FWD: (Loop on hook counts as first st), insert hook into vertical bar of next stitch and pull up a loop, repeat across row to last stitch, insert hook under 2 vertical loops of last stitch and pull up a loop. **RetP:** Yarn over hook, pull through 1 loop on hook, *yarn over hook, pull through 2 loops on hook, repeat from * to end.

Repeat Row 2 to desired length.

Tunisian Purl Stitch (tps)

ROW 1 (RS) FWD: Pull up loop in 2nd ch from hook and each ch across. **RetP:** Yarn over hook, pull through 1 loop on hook, *yarn over hook, pull through 2 loops on hook, repeat from * to end.

ROW 2 FWD: (Loop on hook counts as first stitch), *move yarn to front of work, insert hook into vertical bar of next stitch, yarn over hook, pull up a loop, repeat from * across row to last stitch, insert hook under 2 vertical loops of last stitch and pull up a loop. **RetP:** Yarn over hook, pull through 1 loop on hook, *yarn over, pull through 2 loops on hook, repeat from * to end.

Repeat Row 2 to desired length.

Tunisian Double Crochet (tdc)

FWD: Yarn over hook, insert hook behind vertical bar of stitch as for tss, yarn over hook, pull loop through stitch. Yarn over hook and draw through 2 loops, leaving last loop on hook. **RetP:** Yarn over hook and draw loop through 1 loop on hook, *yarn over hook and draw through 2 loops on hook; repeat from * until 1 loop rem on hook.

Tunisian Knit Single Crochet (tksc)

FWD: Insert hook from front to back between front and back vertical bars and under all horizontal loops of designated stitch, yarn over hook and draw loop through, ch 1. (Sometimes called a Tunisian Extended Stitch Knit-wise, or Corded Stitch.) **RetP:** Yarn over hook, pull through 1 loop on hook, *yarn over hook, pull through 2 loops on hook, repeat from * to end.

Tunisian Single Crochet (tsc)

FWD: Insert hook in designated stitch, yarn over hook and pull up a loop, ch 1. (Sometimes called a Tunisian Extended Stitch.) **RetP:** Yarn over hook, pull through 1 loop on hook, *yarn over hook, pull through 2 loops on hook, repeat from * to end.

embroidery and seaming stitches

Backstitch

Working from right to left, bring needle up at 1 and insert behind the starting point at 2. Bring the needle up at 3, repeat by inserting at 1 and bring the needle up at a point that is a stitch length beyond 3.

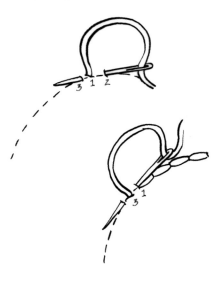

Satin Stitch

Generally worked from left to right, this stitch is used to fill shapes. Bring the needle up at 1, insert at 2, and bring back up at 3. Repeat.

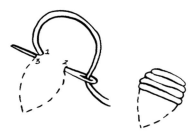

Straight Stitch

Working from right to left, make a straight stitch by bringing the needle up and then inserting ⅛" to ¼" (3 to 6 mm; or longer as necessary) away from the starting point.

Whipstitch Seam

With right sides of work facing and working through edge stitches, bring threaded needle out from back to front, along edge of piece.

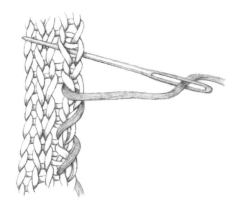

RESOURCES

Blue Sky Alpacas
PO Box 88
Cedar, MN 55011
(763) 753-5815
blueskyalpacas.com
Royal

Brown Sheep Company
100662 County Rd. 16
Mitchell, NE 69357
(800) 826-9136
brownsheep.com
Cotton Fleece; Legacy Lace; Nature-Spun

Caron International
PO Box 222
Washington, NC 27889
caron.com
Naturally Caron Country; Naturally Caron Spa; Simply Soft; Simply Soft Eco

Cascade Yarns
1224 Andover Park E.
Tukwila, WA 98188
cascadeyarns.com
Alpaca Lace Paints; Cascade 220; Heritage

Coats and Clark
PO Box 12229
Greenville, SC 29612
(800) 648-1479
coatsandclark.com
Red Heart Designer Sport; Stitch Nation Alpaca Love; Stitch Nation Full o Sheep

Lion Brand Yarn
135 Kero Rd.
Carlstadt, NJ 07072
(800) 258-9276
lionbrand.com
LB Collection Cotton Bamboo; LB Collection Superwash Merino; LB Collection Wool Stainless Steel; Lion Wool

Tahki/Stacy Charles
70-30 80th St.
Building 36
Ridgewood, NY 11385
(800) 338-9276
tahkistacycharles.com
Filatura Di Crosa Zara Filatura Di Crosa Zarina

Spud and Chloe
(a division of Blue Sky Alpacas)
PO Box 88
Cedar, MN 55011
(888) 460-8862
spudandchloe.com
Fine

INDEX